OUR RUNAWAY AND HOMELESS YOUTH

A Guide to Understanding

Natasha Slesnick

Westport, Connecticut
London

Library of Congress Cataloging-in-Publication Data

Slesnick, Natasha, 1966–
    Our runaway and homeless youth : a guide to understanding / by Natasha Slesnick.
        p. cm.
    Includes bibliographical references and index.
    ISBN 0–275–97994–6
    1. Runaway teenagers—United States. 2. Homeless youth—United States. 3. Parent
and teenager—United States. I. Title.
HV1431.S54 2004
362.74—dc22   2004044373

British Library Cataloguing in Publication Data is available.

Library of Congress Catalog Card Number: 2004044373
ISBN: 0–275–97994–6

First published in 2004

Praeger Publishers, 88 Post Road West, Westport, CT 06881
An imprint of Greenwood Publishing Group, Inc.
www.praeger.com

Printed in the United States of America

The paper used in this book complies with the
Permanent Paper Standard issued by the National
Information Standards Organization (Z39.48–1984).

10   9   8   7   6   5   4   3   2   1

CONTENTS

ACKNOWLEDGMENTS

I am indebted to my mother, Donna, and my sister, Twila, for providing me with direction and insight on this work. Their support and assistance made the completion of this book possible. My father, Irwin, continues to influence me with his joie de vivre and wisdom. Tanya, Trina, and Dan, my other siblings, also teach me what it means to be part of a family. My husband, Rick, is thanked for his patience, humor, and nurturing. I am grateful to my husband for providing diversion to my three children, Dain, Soren, and Tatiana, as I wrote. My energetic and high-spirited children provide me with the experience of unconditional love and joy that undoubtedly influences my work with runaway and homeless children. And finally, the homeless and runaway children and their families with whom I work gave me the inspiration and commitment to complete this book, and for that I am thankful.

INTRODUCTION: WHY A BOOK ON RUNAWAY AND HOMELESS YOUTH?

Our children hold the future in their hands. Some of those children have ice-cold hands, and their own futures do not look bright. These children would prefer to throw their futures away rather than maintain the rules and expectations set for them by their families and others. Some of them are prisoners of their past, unable to escape from their pain. Their futures are not what they wish to hold, and many become troubled adults.

If you are reading this book, you are not seeking entertainment, but information. Perhaps you are the parent of a child who has left home or who is threatening to leave. As a parent, you would like to know more about what you can do to keep your child in the home. Or perhaps you are in the helping profession, and you would like to know more about why children run from home, who these children are, and what happens when they leave. Perhaps you already work with runaways or street youth and want to compare notes. Or, you might just be curious about the lives of street youth. Hopefully, after reading this book you will come away with the sense that all is not hopeless or bleak. Granted, youth homelessness is not a cheery topic. But, the human spirit is strong, as is the drive to connect. Luckily, much healing occurs in the process of connecting with another person.

This book is organized into two sections. Part I is entitled "About Runaway and Homeless Youth." The chapters describe what a runaway is, why children leave home, what such children and their families are like, and what happens to children once they leave home. At the ends of chapters 2,

3, and 4 are stories told by runaway youth (and one by the father of a run-away). Each person relates his or her unique struggles and specific life circumstance. The stories do not characterize all runaways, and you should not assume that all runaways have traumatic and tragic home lives. Nonetheless, the experiences described in these stories are common to many runaways and their families.

Part II of the book is entitled "To the Parents." The first three chapters in this section begin with descriptions of emotions that parents and youth commonly experience under each circumstance. Most youth do not tell their parents how they feel, and parents would probably be surprised by their children's thoughts and emotions. Also, parents might believe that they are alone in their struggles; their frustration, fear, anger, and remorse are immense. Parents might feel less alone when they read that many other parents have similar emotions under similar circumstances. This part provides guidance to parents on what to do when their child leaves, what to do when their child refuses to return home, and what to do when their child does return home. Chapter 8 provides information on how parents can maintain their children in the home (even if the child has never run away). The final chapter in this part describes common scenarios that families with runaway youth might experience. Each scenario is described, along with information about what can be done to address the situation. Parents of runaways often say that service providers do not know how to advise them. Hopefully, this book is a step toward closing this gap.

The guidance presented in the second part of the book is based upon the work I do with street youth as well as with runaway youth and their families. Since 1998 I have provided therapy and trained and supervised other therapists with the goal of uniting runaway youth with their parents—when this goal is appropriate. In addition, since 2000 my colleagues and I have been working with street-living youth whose family situations have disintegrated beyond the point where reintegration is possible. We opened a drop-in center for these homeless youth where they could have respite from the streets to eat, rest, shower, and wash their clothes. They are offered the opportunity to work with a case manager and therapist if they desire. These intervention projects with shelter-residing adolescents and their parents, and with street-living youth have been funded by the National Institutes of Health (National Institute on Alcohol Abuse and Alcoholism and the National Institute on Drug Abuse) and the Department of Health and Human Services (Center for Substance Abuse Treatment).

The goal of these research grants is to develop intervention approaches to serve those who have run away from home or who are homeless teenagers and young adults. No intervention approach has yet been published or is available to guide counselors and families who struggle with this problem. So as a start, I offer the intervention suggestions you find in Part II. These are based upon my work serving 240 families with runaway teenagers and over 200 street-living youth. The information I present to parents is derived from my experiences during these treatment development projects, two of which are the first family-based clinical trials with runaway youth in the country. The intervention used with the runaway youth and their parents was based upon family systems principles, but also upon practical crisis intervention, problem-solving, and communication skills training. These intervention strategies are not new, and their success in effecting positive change has been established in other populations. However, their modification and application to runaway youth and families is new. Though a treatment manual was developed during this project, it is directed to family therapists who work with this population. The information presented in Part II is practical information that parents can use to influence their situation. This material is not meant to be a substitute for family therapy or crisis intervention therapy, but it can be an adjunct to other forms of assistance that families may seek.

Though most people are sympathetic to the plight of runaway and homeless youth and their families, relatively little attention is given to the problem. Rarely do programs serving these kids and their families flourish. Mainstream mental health providers have difficulty addressing the range and intensity of issues found among these families. This is partly due to the lack of information and training available on how best to treat these youth and families. Indeed, the neglect that these youth experience on the street and by those close to them is sadly compounded by societal neglect. Youth homelessness is increasing. Hopefully, with more societal attention and more of us willing to accept a challenge, a situation that appears to be bleak and hopeless can be a tough life experience that makes us all stronger, smarter, and happier.

Part I

ABOUT RUNAWAY AND HOMELESS YOUTH

Chapter 1

WHAT IS A RUNAWAY?

Five thousand children yearly are buried in unmarked graves, either because they are unidentified or unclaimed (Axthelm, 1988). These children were street youth, and their lives prior to reaching the grave would send shivers down the spines of even the most hardened social workers. There is little that a social worker has not heard or seen. Social workers help to redeem our society. They help those who have trouble flourishing—those who have difficulty acquiring the basic needs of food, housing, clothing, and medical and mental health care. A child who can shock a social worker is a child who has seen more than a child should see, and has more to say than most children.

Some basic needs social workers cannot fill, and these needs are pronounced among children. They need love, care, and supervision. However, some runaway adolescents interpret love as a father who shares his marijuana ("He respects me as a man and a friend") or a mother who slaps her child hard across the face when the child fails a class ("That means she loves me and cares about my future"). Their world may surprise, sadden, or even revolt some people. If ignorance is bliss, then the good news is that most young children do not know a different life. A life of pain, indifference, conflict, or abuse is a familiar life, a known life, their sole life. Only in talking with other people—at school, at church, or in the neighborhood—do they begin to learn that perhaps, just maybe, their familiar, comfortable life may not be the lives that others have. For some kids, this realization leads to options. And as will be shown, a few kids chose their own options, while others have their options chosen for them.

The human condition is composed of many emotions and experiences. A healthy, functioning family, supportive friends, warmth, compassion, security, and freedom from hunger are perhaps one end of the continuum. We are also made up of experiences from the other end of the continuum, including desperation, loneliness, fear, selfishness, hunger, violence, and victimization. A street youth may expose some of her listeners to experiences or sides of the human condition that the listener never thought existed, or did not wish to admit existed.

Who are the listeners? A listener can be anyone who comes into contact with a street kid. Some listeners are seeking to assist the youth—counselors, social workers, nurses, clergy. These people may seek out homeless kids to talk with. Usually, the helping listeners seek kids out in order to encourage them to come to a program or church to get food and rest. A listener may be someone just walking by a panhandling street kid. The conversation may start with the listener asking, "How are you doing?" Listeners might also be police officers who pick up the kids and take them to the juvenile justice center, or probation officers. A listener can be anyone. Granted, anyone willing to take the time to listen to the story of a street kid is going to leave the conversation feeling different than they did before the conversation.

Probably, the most consistent listeners to street kids are those seeking to help them. When first beginning to work with street youth, listening to their stories, a new counselor often reports feeling overwhelmed or emotionally drained. Youths' stories are painful; their emotions are raw and sometimes childlike or untamed. Some counselors struggle with the urge to take care of the youth. Counselors want to take the kids home with them, feed them, take them to school, and get them involved in after-school activities. They want them to be like other kids. The counselor wants to remove the children's pain, pluck them from the streets and put them back where they belong—right into the middle of mainstream society. Inevitably, supervision with the new counselor starts with the counselor stating, "I can't believe what she said happened to her. It's awful, I just can't believe it." The counselor's reaction is normal. Children should not be experiencing rape, hunger, trauma, or beatings by adult pimps. They shouldn't have to feel as though no one really cares about them.

Listening is the first step to healing. In the end, the counselors, social workers, and clergy cannot simply give the child a new life, but must help youth build their own new lives. Through listening, a counselor's unwavering positive regard and patience in building trust can be rewarded with a positive relationship with a street youth. A connection with a homeless youth is a precious connection. It is not easily made, and it can have a profound impact on the child and even the therapist. Trust is a significant barrier to working with runaway and homeless street youth. By the time many youth get to the streets, they have lost faith in mainstream society and adults in general. Too many people have given up on them. They have been told too many times that they are no good. Many youth and parents have been through the system, finding that ultimately they are not understood and cannot be helped. This is exemplified by the high percentage of youth who drop out of system care prematurely (63%) (McMillan & Tucker, 1999). Some youth report being betrayed by those they trust. For example, a child may have felt betrayed by a parent who said, "You cannot live here any longer." Many youth report feeling betrayed by parents who did not believe their reports of sexual abuse by parents and/or stepparents. And, we cannot forget system betrayal. Some children who are removed from the home and placed into foster care suffer even worse abuse at the hands of strangers. The average number of placements for older teenagers in the system is reported to be 7.59 (McMillan & Tucker, 1999).

A trusting relationship with an adult works to repair a child's lost trust in other people. Most of us expect our parents to allow us more latitude than our friends or even our lovers. Our parents are supposed to come close to providing the unconditional love that is described in storybooks and Shakespeare's sonnets. Our parents provide us a template for what to expect in other people and in life. They are our primary agents in preparing us for dealing with others. When the parent or the child says he or she can no longer be in a relationship with the other, havoc is wrought upon the young person's worldview. Of course, the child learns that no one can be trusted and that a love relationship is a relationship filled with pain and rejection. No one in his or her right mind would want that! So, a youth who is severed from his or her parents' positive regard is not likely to enthusiastically dive into close relationships. Understandably, these kids often avoid such relationships. Youth who have chosen, or have been told, to leave home learn to hone their survival skills. And if they are to survive, they learn not to trust. Lack of trust protects them from further rejection and abandonment. This is one of their first survival lessons in life.

Unfortunately, runaway youth's fear, loneliness, and anger are intense. Fortunately, just as intense is the drive to connect with someone and feel cared about, to love and be loved, even in the face of utter rejection and abandonment. Starvation for street kids comes in many forms, and physical hunger is only one form, perhaps one of the least significant. In the end, humans are more similar to one another than they are different. This allows us to empathize with someone who is seemingly nothing like us. A homeless youth mirrors our worst nightmare: rejection by those we love, and seemingly constant pain, desperation, and solitude. These are not new emotions for most people. In fact, they are emotions that most of us have experienced to a greater or lesser degree but prefer to avoid. This makes us similar to street kids.

In time, therapists, social workers, counselors, teachers, and clergy learn to listen to stories of suffering with some degree of equanimity. This is not to say that they no longer care or have become hardened to tragedy. All new information, experiences, and intense emotions require energy to organize. A person needs to figure out how those new thoughts and emotions fit in with their current experience of the world. When the world shows a new side, it has to be dealt with and incorporated into the person's worldview. That is not to say the experience is no longer appreciated, only that it is no longer a shock.

One can understand suffering as part of a broad set of human experiences. The suffering of street youth is not a finite, static experience. If that were the case, no therapist, no social worker, no parent, no clergy, or no teacher would continue in the quest to serve our runaway and homeless children and their families. Great suffering and desperation can lead to sweeter peace and contentment, sweeter because one who has suffered greatly can appreciate the lack of suffering far better than one who has not suffered so greatly.

Just as human experience is varied, with a range of experiences and emotions, individuals with shared experiences are varied as well. There is no such thing as a typical alcoholic or a typical depressed person. Indeed, alcoholics share a dependence on alcohol, and depressed individuals report similar feelings of sadness and hopelessness associated with major depressive disorder. Yet, the development, course, and resolution of depression are different among individuals. Similarly, not all runaway and homeless youth and their families are alike. They share a disconnection with other family members and perhaps the broader social system. Runaway and homeless youth and their families are as different from one another as are individuals riding a subway. Not all families are abusive, and not all runaways are lost, angry, or mentally ill.

Early work with runaway youth focused on classifying runaways into various typologies and documenting their associated problem behaviors. The literature on treating runaway youth is more remarkable for what we do not know than for what we do know, and it has been noted that runaway and homeless youth are an underserved and understudied population (e.g.,

Rotheram-Borus, Feldman, Rosario, & Dunne, 1994). To date, the bulk of information on runaway and homeless youth has been obtained from street and shelter surveys. In a street survey, an interviewer goes to popular hangouts where homeless youth are known to be, often as part of an agency's regular outreach efforts. Interviewers ask kids to fill out questionnaires, or may ask them to answer a set of structured, interviewer-administered questions. In most cases, the youth are compensated for the time spent completing the survey.

Information about runaway and homeless youth is also obtained through drop-in centers or shelters where youth may go to receive food, clothing, or sanctuary from the streets. Drop-in centers often have demographic data sheets for youth to complete when they enter the center. These sheets instruct youth to mark their age, gender, ethnicity, and other nonidentifying information. In shelters, where some youth may go to receive temporary housing, shelter staff members typically have long interviews with the youth.

When digesting information about street youth, some factors need to be considered. Youth have reported that in order to receive compensation for completing street surveys, they will ensure a match to the interviewer's requirement for eligibility. That is, if the interviewer is seeking drug-abusing street youth, the youth will state that they use drugs, even if they never have, in order to be eligible to complete the survey. Ten dollars is a lot of money for a homeless youth. If a youth is willing to have sex for money or put his or her life on the line to sell drugs to earn a living, then answering a few questions for ten bucks is almost too good to be true, and certainly too good to pass up. Another factor to consider when evaluating information about street youth is the trust barrier. If the youth is fearful of being identified because she does not want her parents or social worker contacted, then the accuracy of information provided in surveys can be questioned.

WHAT EXACTLY ARE WE TALKING ABOUT?

The terms *runaway* and *homeless* can be confusing. Youth homelessness is defined by the U.S. Department of Health and Human Services (1999, p. 300) as "a situation in which a youth has no place of shelter and is in need of services and a shelter where he or she can receive supervision and care." A child who has left home, sleeps inside a city drainpipe during the day, stays awake at night for protection, and eats using money earned by panhandling is certainly homeless. This child is in need of shelter where he or she can receive supervision and care. A child who leaves home and stays at a friend's home would not meet this definition for homeless. That child is not in need of shelter and is likely to be receiving supervision and care. Although the child staying at a friend's home is not homeless, she meets the definition of a runaway youth. A runaway youth is defined as being "away from home without the permission of his or her parents or legal guardian or is absent from home or place of legal residence at least overnight without permission" (U.S. Department of Health and Human Services, 1999a, p. 300; see also 1999b).

In addition to the Department of Health and Human Services' definition, among those who work with runaway youth and their families, *runaway* is used to denote a youth who has left home voluntarily. These youth may have planned their departures—perhaps packed a bag, joined a boyfriend or a girlfriend with plans to leave the city, and saved up money. Leaving home involved a decision process and planning. In addition, there are chronic and acute runaways. A chronic runaway will leave and return home many times over the course of a year or several years. A youth may have an acute runaway episode. An acute episode may be that the youth left home once and stayed away for a long period of time. Such youth may return home and never leave again, or they may never return home.

Throwaways or *pushouts* are evicted by their families, often following extensive conflict with their parents. These youth have been told that they may no longer live in the home and must leave. Estimates of throwaways range from 9.3 percent to 33 percent among shelter and street surveyed youth (Ringwalt, Greene, & Robertson, 1998; Rotheram-Borus, 1993). Throwaway youth experience more violence and conflict with their families than do runaways (Finkelhor, Hotaling, & Sedlak, 1990). Many gay and lesbian youth are rejected by their families and forced to leave home (Kruks, 1991). In New York, estimates are that as many as half of youth on the streets are gay or lesbian (Humm, 1990), while 40 percent of the homeless youths in Seattle are estimated to be gay (Seattle Department of Human Resources, 1988). Parents of these youth are unable to tolerate their child's sexual orientation and so remove the child from the home. Throwaways report more severe alcohol and drug use and related problem behaviors than do other youth who are no longer in the home. These kids are at greater risk for victimization while on the streets and are at greater risk for HIV, hepatitis, and sexually transmitted diseases, given unprotected sexual practices and intravenous drug use (Johnson, Aschkenasy, Herbers, & Gillenwater, 1996).

Children expect acceptance and love from their parents, and most have great difficulty dealing with the situation when a parent breaks the rules by not providing love or care to the child's satisfaction. In child abuse shelters, four- and five-year-old children are dropped off by the police because of the abuse they suffered at the hands of their parents. These children's parents may have burned them with cigarettes, raped them, or locked them in closets for hours on end. At night, while staying in the shelter, some of these children cry for their parents, "I want my mommy!" In the morning, they ask when they get to go home. Why? Because they love their parents. A child does not know that love does not come in the form of emotional and physical pain. Questions such as "Why don't they love me?" or "What's wrong with me?" become the building blocks of how they learn to think of themselves. When a child believes that he or she is worthless and that no one cares, that child will expect to be treated badly by others and will not expect much for himself or herself. Children who grow up with these ideas about themselves and with the early experience of painful love will more likely accept abusive relationships with lovers. These grown children may also be comfortable working at jobs that require markedly lower skills than they are truly capable of, with significantly lower pay. As adults, they tell themselves that this is love, this is life, this is what I deserve.

System kids have been shuffled back and forth among foster homes, psychiatric hospitals, emergency shelters, residential schools, and juvenile justice facilities (Shaffer & Caton, 1984). These youth are system savvy. They may have psychological and legal jargon down and talk with their therapists, social workers, or probation officers about the various diagnoses that they have been assigned. These children know the rules of the system, the laws, and in some cases their legal rights. Studies of homeless youth consistently find large proportions (on average, 50%) with histories of multiple agency placements (Athey, 1995).

A differentiation may also be made between street kids and shelter kids. *Street kids* make their lives on the streets. They survive as best they can under extreme circumstances. They may squat in abandoned buildings— break into a building and make it their temporary home. Some street kids sleep on roofs, in doorways, under bridges, in parks, in cars, or in hotels, or with anyone who will provide shelter and warmth for the night. Perhaps they have negotiated an exchange of services for their temporary stay. For example, *survival sex* is the exchange of sexual favors for food, shelter, clothing, or even drugs. Some kids exchange drugs for a night's stay in someone's home. Survival skills are taught by other street youth. A street kid may hook up with other street kids for protection and for the purpose of learning the rules of the street.

Shelter kids may never have spent a night on the streets. These youth will go to a shelter after going from one friend's home to another, and wearing out their welcome. Some youth end up in shelters after they are arrested and their parents refuse to allow them back into the home. In these cases, the police transport the youth to the shelter when they are released from juvenile detention. Some parents drop their kids off at the shelter in order to get a break from raising them. A child may be placed in a shelter if his or her family is under investigation for abuse or neglect. Shelter kids do not consider themselves homeless and may never have the experience of living on the streets. Some youth have always had shelter and appropriate supervision and care.

The terms just discussed are useful for categorizing the types of kids who are out of the home. But the terms can be confusing given the complexity of reasons that youth leave home. A street kid may also be a runaway or a pushout. A street kid may also have been a system kid and never a runaway. How about the street youth who was pushed out of his family's home, was then shuffled around in the system to various group homes, and ran away from the most recent foster care placement? That street youth has been a throwaway, a system, and a runaway youth.

EXTENT OF THE PROBLEM

It is hard to say how many kids are living on the street on any given night. Census and household surveys do not include runaway and street kids, as these children usually take extended absences from school and do not have residences to be tracked to by those conducting the surveys. Because of the crudeness in estimating the number of runaway and street youth, estimates range from 500,000 to 4 million children yearly who leave home (Athey, 1995; Klein et al., 2000). This is a large range; it is like saying that the chances of rain tomorrow range from 10 percent to 100 percent. There is no accurate account of how many kids run away from home, or how many are on the streets. Many estimates are taken from agencies that serve runaway youth. However, most homeless youth will not access services in the community, so large numbers of youth will not be included in those counts.

One child in eight is expected to leave home prior to age 18. If the home is headed by a single parent, or if there are more than eight persons living in the home, then one in four children are estimated to leave home prior to reaching age 18 (Kurtz, Jarvis, & Kurtz, 1991). These estimates suggest that a runaway child is not a rare child. It is not clear why the rate would double in single-parent families and in families with more than eight persons. Possibly, single-parent and large families are under more stress, socially and financially. Fewer social supports such as friends and family, isolation, and relatively little money make it much more difficult for parents to successfully address adolescent and family problems. If a mother is working two jobs to keep the household going, it is hard to come home to a third job—parenting. If this parent is alone without someone to assist in parenting, exhaustion and stress from working all day is not alleviated when she or he returns home. If anything, it may increase! Children need more than to be fed and clothed. They also are a whirlwind of needs and emotions. These needs for closeness and attention make themselves known in all sorts of different ways. A mother may return home and a child may run to the door crying, "I'm hungry, I'm hungry! Where have you been?! I want dinner NOW!" The mother may muster all the restraint she has to calmly respond, "Just give me a minute to put my things down and check the mail." And the mother hopes that the child has developed enough empathy to understand that she is on the verge of hopping a jet plane for Aruba for a much-needed vacation. More likely, the response she will receive is, "But Mommmmmaaaaa, I'm *HUNGRY*." Single-parent households and households in which the children outnumber the adults by four to one simply have many more demands placed upon the parents and children. The parents are required to maintain the home and meet the requirements of child rearing, including completing school-related tasks, disciplining, meeting the children's basic needs, and nurturing the children. Children in large households or homes with one parent may need to increase their level of responsibility in the home more quickly than other children. They may also need to work harder to get the attention that they require from the parent(s), and some may not get their needs completely met.

Though our estimates of the number of youth on the streets vary widely, we do know that, like homeless families, homeless youths are increasing in number (Kurtz, Jarvis, & Kurtz, 1991), with estimated increases in homelessness ranging from 10 to 38 percent annually. Shelters do not have enough available bed space to accommodate the number of youth requesting services. And we also know that most kids who leave home do not even go to shelters (U.S. House of Representatives, 1992). Not uncommonly, those children most in need of help will not request it.

TREATMENT: WHAT WE KNOW

We know very little about how to help runaway and homeless youth and their family. Other than an HIV and case management intervention with street youth (Cauce et al., 1994; Rotheram-Borus, Koopman, Haignere, & Davies, 1991), no published reports were found that identify effective treatment interventions with homeless youth. Shelters and shelter-based programs have been the only interventions noted in the literature, and virtually no data exist that specify the treatment received by youth while in these shelters (Teare et al., 1994). There are over 300 runaway shelters across the United States that receive federal funding through Title III of the Juvenile Justice and Delinquency Prevention Act of 1974. A nationwide survey of 185 agencies offering shelter to runaway and homeless youth found that these agencies provided, on average, 14 different services to their clients (National Network of Runaway and Youth Services, 1991). Shelters that receive federal funding are supposed to alleviate the problems of runaway youth. These problems include reuniting kids with their families, encouraging stable living conditions, and helping youth decide what to do once they leave the shelter. Shelters are overcrowded, and many shelters do not have staff trained to deal with youth who have substance abuse and mental health problems (Grigsby, 1992). Unfortunately, many runaway youth have ongoing substance abuse and mental health issues—not all runaway youth, but many. Most shelters will not accept youth known to have histories of serious substance abuse or mental health problems. This is due primarily to liability issues, and for the safety of other children. Shelters often function on limited funding. They have just enough to keep the doors open and a skeleton staff on the payroll to monitor the youth. Youth who require detoxification from alcohol or drugs, or have histories of serious mental illness require more staff resources. The kids who need more attention and help are usually the kids on the streets. Street kids will usually avoid shelters. If they do seek help at a shelter, chances are they will not be accepted into the program; or if they are accepted, they will be discharged early.

In sum, shelters are the primary intervention noted for runaway youth, and we do not know exactly what shelters are providing to youth or how effective their interventions are. In order to determine this, shelters need to document the services they provide to the kids and then track the kids over time to see if their behavior stabilized and improved. Unfortunately, this requires time and resources. Time, and more importantly resources, are scarce commodities in youth shelters. Funding is often tenuous, and it is always less than what is needed to provide the range and intensity of services that youth and their families really need.

Many treatments are available to adults who suffer from a range of ailments, including depression, phobias and other anxiety disorders, manic depression, and substance abuse. This can be verified by browsing the local bookstore. Much information about parenting is available. However, treatment guides addressing problems associated with runaway youth and their families are nonexistent. There are several reasons for this. Runaway youth and their families are known by mental health workers to be difficult to engage and maintain in treatment. Mental health workers' inability to maintain runaway youth and families in treatment hampers the ability of treatment programs to be evaluated and guidelines for providers to be developed. If a family comes in for one or two sessions and never returns, then clearly the therapy did not do its job. On the other hand, a youth and/or his or her family might come in to 15 sessions and change nothing. That treatment did not do its job either. But to know whether the treatment did its job, agencies have to assess what is going on in the family before treatment starts, and then find the family after the treatment has been completed and question them. If things are going better at the end of treatment than at the beginning then something, probably the treatment, helped.

No treatment has yet been developed that can effectively engage and address the problems associated with runaway youth and their families. If the treatments that these families received were helping, the family might continue coming to sessions. Perhaps it is not the family that is difficult to engage and help. Perhaps the family does not see that the treatment is worth coming to. In other words, treatment providers may not know how best to engage and help these families... yet.

Families may receive treatment through several sources. First, some families are introduced into the system when the Children, Youth, and Families Department has been notified about potential neglect and/or physical and sexual abuse within the family. When Child Protective Services gets involved with a family, members are often court ordered to participate in treatment, which usually consists of a combination of individual and family therapy. Second, some kids who run away from home get arrested and through interactions with their local juvenile justice system also are court ordered into treatment with their family. Third, runaways do not often maintain school attendance when they have left home. When the child returns to school, he or she may meet with a school counselor who may also recommend that the family receive counseling. Alternatively, youth may be reported to the truancy officer, and the juvenile justice center may become involved that way. And, of course, some families seek assistance voluntarily, without external prodding from the State Children, Youth, and Families Department, the juvenile justice center, or the public school system.

Families and youth are also introduced to the system through youth shelters. When youth are placed in a youth shelter or go there voluntarily, the family is often in a state of crisis. During a crisis, these youth and families are sometimes more willing to accept help than at other times (Rohr & James, 1994). A family is more likely to give therapy a chance when family members have reached their wit's end. When no matter what they do, nothing seems to get better in the family, a mother may think, "Certainly, things could not get worse than they already are." This presents a unique opportunity to members of the helping profession. Youth who go to shelters, unlike many, are asking for help. And usually, they still have families that are willing to work on the problems that are in front of them. Most kids who go to shelters return home—98 percent of them. These families still have a chance to reunite and stay reunited. If the youth is legally able to go home from the shelter, engaging parents in counseling is almost always the right thing to do. The youth ran from a family situation; he or she did not run away in order to add excitement to life. Thus, family problems are a large part of the reason that the youth left home. In order to address the situation successfully, the entire family is needed (Rohr & James, 1994). It is difficult to address family problems without having the entire family present. That is like trying to operate on a leg and cutting the leg off from the rest of the body in order to fix it.

Without help to manage family conflict and expectations for one another, children may return home only to leave again after the first fight. A youth shelter can serve an important function for families. It can connect families to other services in a community. If shelter staff cannot provide family therapy, they usually have staff who will help the family get into counseling with a different agency. The worst-case scenario is that the family does not receive treatment or is unable to manage the situation itself. Then, when the child leaves home again, he or she does not return to the shelter, but goes straight to the streets. That child has given up on both the family and the system.

After several years of being tossed around the system, families and kids might become system resistant. The biggest sign of system resistance is when parents say that they have already been through therapy, the therapy did not help them, and so they do not want to waste their or the counselor's time again. Families that experience system burnout are often families that required more support than the system was able to manage. Perhaps the parents need marital therapy, or the child needs assistance in school and in finding after-school activities. In addition, the other children in the home have their own struggles, including problems with the juvenile justice system or friends who smoke pot and steal. Families that continue to have problems and continue to need support are the families that are most disenchanted with the system and with mental health services.

The goal of service providers should then be to intervene early, when the family has not yet lost faith in others' ability to help them (Slesnick, Meyers, Meade, & Segelken, 2000). Although not a treatment developed specifically for families with runaway youth, one program was developed to maintain youth in the home, with the goal of preventing children from being removed to foster care. The prototypical intensive family preservation service program, Homebuilders was started by clinical psychologists in 1974 to provide an alternative to foster care and institutional placement of children in Washington state (Kinney, Haapala, Madsen, & Fleming, 1977). Homebuilders family preservation services are based on crisis intervention theory, which postulates that a family is most open to change when it is faced with a crisis and its normal modes of coping no longer work (Barth, 1990). The program was structured to provide immediate, intensive services over a brief time period. This approach includes three assumptions: (1) time-limited, intensive, and comprehensive therapeutic services should be provided in accordance with the needs and priorities of each family; (2) most children are better off with their own families than in substitute care; and (3) services to avert placement outside the home should be funded at the same level as placement.

In most cases, the family's crisis is precipitated by the threat of removal of a child by Child Protective Services, usually because of abuse or neglect. Appointments are scheduled at the client's convenience, often in the evenings and, for the most part, in the family's home; counselors are available around the clock for crisis calls. In-home services are seen as providing more accurate information about family strengths and problems and an opportunity to model and practice new behaviors in the client's natural environment (Nelson & Landsman, 1992).

Homebuilders works. In general, families receiving therapy with the Homebuilders program had fewer out-of-home placements than did comparison groups for samples of youth in juvenile justice, child welfare, and mental health programs who did not receive family preservation services (Nelson, 1994). Not only did families who received these services have a greater chance of staying together (9 percent to 38 percent were placed outside the home, compared to 72 percent to 100 percent in comparison groups), but family members also showed significant improvements in family functioning, parenting, and child performance when treatment was completed (Feldman, 1991).

The family preservation model has the same conceptual base as the multisystemic treatment model, where severe behavior problems associated with runaway youth are considered to be determined by many, many things and are best addressed in corresponding areas (Henggeler et al., 1991). Whereas traditional forms of family therapy focus almost completely on the parent–adolescent interaction, multisystemic approaches meet with both the adolescent and parent together, alone, or with other family members such as grandparents and aunts. Meeting alone with family members is done so that individual issues, such as problems with coping, parenting, or anger management, may be addressed with the therapist.

Wonderful: We have an intervention for families that are on the verge of being broken apart. So let family preservation therapy begin early in system involvement to prevent further problems! This sounds logical. It seems like a good idea. There is always a hang-up, and the hang-up here is that home-based therapy is expensive. It costs a lot of money to send a therapist to a client's house and to meet with the client several times weekly for several months. Plus, these therapists do more than therapy. They also do case management, which involves setting up appointments with other agencies and assisting families get to those appointments if needed. Yet, in the end, the social expense of pushing a child through the system is far greater than the expense of conducting intensive family preservation therapy prior to the child's being removed from the home.

To this point, we have discussed what to do if the family is still in the life of the youth. In some cases, the family is no longer involved in the youth's life, and the youth wants no contact with his or her parents. Sometimes this is the best choice for all involved. The family is supposed to serve as the primary agent of healthy socialization for its children. Family relationships can disintegrate to the point where they no longer serve the function they were supposed to serve. Family members do not support or guide other members, and unconditional positive regard either never existed or was replaced with anger, rage, resentment, or worse, indifference.

If the youth is on the streets, reunification with the family is difficult, and intervention with the youth alone should take priority. If a youth chooses sleeping on the streets over any other alternative, then he or she has made a significant choice. Not many of us would easily give up a home with food, warmth, and clothes. A home would have to be more than unpleasant for a child to decide to no longer live with parent(s) and siblings. Who would rather live in doorways, under bridges, in abandoned buildings, or in crowded hotel rooms with other kids? Who would chose to take a chance on being hungry, or getting sick and having no access to medical care? When on the street, you cannot just find a nice warm door-way and snooze away. Many street kids stay awake at night and sleep during the day so that they do not get physically attacked, robbed, or harassed by emotionally unstable older street people. When children leave home for the streets, it means that they would rather deal with all that the streets involve than deal with their families. They would rather deal with the streets than deal with shelters and the system. That says a lot about their families, and it says a lot about the system.

Intervening in the lives of street youth is not without its own challenges (Morrissette, 1992; Smart & Ogborne, 1994). It is difficult for kids to keep appointments when living on the street. Things come up, unscheduled things—like when the police raid the hotel in which they are staying, and they have to get their stuff out and find another place to sleep that night. Or, they get into a fight with someone and are so injured that they cannot move. A kid did not make it to her appointment because the trick she had the night before took her to the outskirts of town, raped her, and beat her so badly that she was left for dead. In this instance, the counselor heard from another street youth that an elderly couple, on a walk, found her and called the police. In the end, she was taken to the hospital, so the next therapy appointment with her was in the hospital. Many kids have appointment books; it is not always that they forget their appointments. Appointments are just hard to keep sometimes.

These children do not have a residence or phone number at which to contact them if they miss an appointment. The counselor is at their mercy. Youth who do not want to continue in therapy, or do not trust their counselor or social worker, do not come back. The counselor will never hear from them again. In usual practice, most counselors will call a client who misses his or her therapy appointment(s). During this call, the counselor will try to reengage the client into treatment and, at the very least, ask that the client return for one more session—to say good-bye. On the other hand, if the child experiences the counselor (or case manager, therapist, or social worker) as someone who can be trusted, the child will be back. If the counselor provides hope to the child or gives the child a peek at normalcy and compassion, the child will be back. He or she may not return at the scheduled time. He or she may call three hours after the scheduled appointment stating that he or she is across the city but would still like to meet. This is a child who is becoming connected again, who is beginning to care.

When working with homeless street youth, mental health issues take a back seat to survival issues at the beginning. Food, shelter, clothing, and medical care are priorities over assistance with depression or psychosis and longer-term plans and goals. Who wants to talk about an anxiety disorder when his or her stomach is cramping from starvation or an impacted tooth is oozing into his or her mouth? It is hard to get a job when you do not have an address, a place to shower, and food to eat.

Alcohol and drug use relieves kids temporarily. Without hope, security, a plan, and a will to live a different life, it is fruitless to take away the youth's sole means of escape and coping. Homeless adults will say that they started using drugs because the drugs provided many positive side effects. For example, drugs helped them forget their past and present, calmed them, or kept them from feeling depressed. Eventually, the drugs become a physical necessity, just like food. No longer were drugs taken to get a high, but instead were used to prevent sickness (from withdrawal). So, in time the drugs become the problem as well. Most street youth have not gotten to the point where drugs are recognized as a problem. Some kids even start off their first session by saying, "If you try to tell me to stop using drugs, you'll be wasting your time."

Chapter 2

WHY CHILDREN LEAVE HOME

A counselor who could see into the future and know which child in which family will run away from home under which circumstances would be widely sought indeed. Perhaps that savvy counselor hides a magical therapy crystal ball. Imagine the grand therapeutic deeds that could be done with such a view into the future! We know a little about why some kids leave home for the unknown. Most of what we know is told to us by street kids. We cannot know what *causes* youth homelessness because no one has done a study to determine that. If we knew *why* some youth leave home and others never leave, we could predict who will run and under what circumstances. With this information, counselors and social workers could target those at risk before they ever leave the family. Even if the child has already left home, counselors would be in a much better position to aid the family when the child returns; she would know what problems in the family to address, and what strengths to foster in order to keep the child at home. Such a targeted intervention is bound to have better client outcomes than an intervention without specific targets.

Pondering *why* some kids run away from home and some kids do not can actually take you down some interesting roads. Take for example, two children in the same family, Soren and Dain. Each child is treated fairly equally by the parents. Soren tends to sulk when he does not get his way, while Dain yells and stomps. When the rules are laid down, Soren grumbles but will follow them. Dain rebels and sneaks out at night when he does not agree with the rules or when he thinks the punishment is unjust.

Eventually, Dain gets caught sneaking out and gets grounded for two weeks. Still, he continues to sneak out of the house. Sometimes he returns to his bed at 3:00 A.M. without anyone else in the family knowing. Other times he gets caught. With the conflict and tension in the family increasing, Dain eventually stays out with his friends for an entire night. A high-spirited independent quality, in combination with friends who encourage freedom seeking, leads to a runaway episode for Dain. Soren, an easygoing rule follower, does not like to break the rules and never sneaks out of the house or runs away from home. Thus, two children in the same environment follow disparate paths in response to their shared family environment.

Running away from home is likely related to many family, social, individual, and peer variables. Personality variables, such as shyness or dependence, or having few friends or connections outside the family may prevent one youth from leaving home even in the face of sadistic, violent abuse. Another child with characteristics of independence and defiance, as well as camaraderie with peers, may leave home without ever having experienced violence, sexual abuse, or neglect.

THE FAMILY SITUATION

Many new therapists working with runaway children and their families have arrived at supervision and exclaimed, "I don't know why this adolescent [for instance, Tatiana] ran away from home; everything in the family seems really normal! The parents say there are no big problems, and Tatiana says that the family is great. The mom and dad say they have no idea why Tatiana left home, except that she wanted to stay out late with her friends. When I asked them about family conflict, they say they don't fight with each other and they get along really well." The fledgling therapist might even recommend to the supervisor that the family not continue in therapy. The therapist might assert that the family "seems to have things under control," and that the runaway episode was just one of those rebellious things kids do.

Resolution of this situation requires a delicate approach. The experienced supervisor knows that an adolescent who runs away from home is invoking the ultimate move in a very tense high-stakes game of chess. Running away from home is similar to threatening suicide. Some theoreticians have noted that, among those suffering from depression, the threat of suicide is the only way out of an interactional stalemate with loved ones (Coyne, 1976). Over time, messages of helplessness and hopelessness from depressed individuals fall upon unsympathetic ears. The messages from a depressed person have to become more intense in order to have the unmet needs for love and reassurance filled. The care and love messages received prior to the suicide threat or attempt were no longer perceived as sincere, just as the people in the depressed person's life have become hardened to their loved one's depression over time. Tearfulness, lethargy, and gloom elicit annoyance rather than compassion over a course of six months. Attempted or threatened suicide elicits real compassion and care again. A suicide attempt thus creates closeness again.

The child is in a situation with his parents where, no matter what he does, nothing in the family changes for the better. He tries everything from arguing, sneaking out, and sulking, but problems remain. He does not feel safe, supported, or heard. Once he feels that he has tried everything, only one thing is left: leaving the family behind. For some families, this is enough to evoke change. The parents may search the streets and find the child walking along the street with other raggedy-looking kids. They do not recognize him at first because he looks dirty, he looks tough, and he is smoking a cigarette. Finally, they realize the seriousness of the problem; his complaints and requests for family change may be heard; and the family goes into therapy.

Running away from home is not a developmentally expected behavior in adolescence. Teenagers do not leave home when things are going well. Teenagers do not leave home because they do not like the rules, or because they did not take the trash out when they were supposed to. They do not run away because they wanted to go to a party and their parents told them no. Teenagers leave home, or are told to leave, when something is seriously wrong at home (Whitbeck & Hoyt, 1999). It is not one or two things; it is many things over a long period of time. As a local street youth said when interviewed by a television reporter, "We don't end up on the streets because we have a Beaver Cleaver family or because we didn't do our homework. We end up on the streets because things were really messed up at home."

Family Support

Recently, researchers have provided evidence that adolescents are running from something rather than running to something (Whitbeck & Hoyt, 1999). Primarily, kids are running from troubles within a family. Runaways rate their families as having more problems than do families with nonrunaways (Whitbeck & Hoyt, 1999). As children develop into adolescence, other influences (e.g., peer) increase, but for most children, the family remains a major source of guidance and support in the child's life.

Lack of a supportive family might be the single largest factor associated with adolescent homelessness (Rotheram-Borus, 1991). Runaway youth report that their families provided little support to them. Even the parents of runaway youth, compared with parents of nonrunaway youth, report that they provided less support and more rejection to their children (Whitbeck & Hoyt, 1999). Are parents of runaway youth just unloving, bad parents? No. Parents of runaway youth have their own struggles. Exhaustion strikes some parents who have many children in the home; others work two jobs in order to meet the family's basic needs. When parents use most of their time and energy to meet the basic needs of their children, then it follows that providing for the emotional needs of the children lags behind.

If a particular child does not require a large amount of support from his parent(s), he might still thrive in the home. Perhaps he receives support from other adults in his life, or even from other brothers and sisters. An older sibling who can help a child with homework or give advice when needed might fulfill that child's needs for parental support. Even a friend's parent with whom he feels comfortable and who takes an active interest in his life might satisfy his need for parental guidance.

A child who needs a close parental relationship may not flourish, and his demands may create conflict. We know that frequent arguing is characteristic of families with youth who leave home (Slesnick & Meade, 2001). Problems often occur when the match between the child's needs and the parents' needs are at odds, and reconciliation is difficult.

A possible scenario: Two people have met and fallen in love. The first three months are a flurry of compliments, attention, fun, and laughter. As the flush of new love moves to the stage of working together to meet life's struggles and daily hassles, then an evaluation takes place. Each person in the relationship has a set of needs and expectations for the other. Some couples meet each other's needs easily. Other couples find it more difficult. Perhaps one person needs lots of reassurance about his place in the other's heart. Perhaps one needs alone time that the other cannot give without resentment. For some of these couples with disparate needs, the relationship ends, and the partners again begin searching for that perfect match.

If the relationship continues, children may be born into a couple's life. Children do not get to pick and chose a good match. Some children mirror their parents' personalities, and their needs requirements complement one another. Other children are born with very different personalities and emotional needs from their parents. Unlike a romantic love relationship, when the match is not complementary, the child cannot easily leave, nor can the parent.

Flexibility in the Face of Change

Some parents have difficulty coping with normal developmental changes in their child. Adolescence is a time of independence seeking. The teen explores different ideas and attitudes with the underlying purpose of defining who he or she is. Parents with rigid expectations for their child's behavior might have difficulty adapting to the changes they see in their child. Perhaps their son wants to wear baggy clothes and does not want to go to church anymore. Maybe he wants to stay out later on the weekend or has a girlfriend and spends less time at home. Or perhaps he begins to say things that the parents do not agree with—that he wants drugs legalized, for example. The rules for an 8-year-old must be different from the rules for a 14-year-old. Parenting, though it should remain a benevolent dictatorship, must include more negotiation with the child as he gets older. Trouble begins when parents have difficulty adapting to normal developmental demands for increased independence by their child.

Just as some parents have difficulty with change, so do some kids. Some youth do not like the men their mother dates. Sometimes the mother's boyfriend has children of his own who come to the house. Not only must the child now share his mother with the boyfriend, but also with the boyfriend's children. Granted, this is a difficult situation for any youth. However, some youth have more trouble than others adapting to new situations.

Communication

Though all families with children must cope with change of one sort or another, some families are able to cope better than others. Some families are flexible; they go with the flow. Some families always sit down together for meals and use that time to discuss things that happened during the day. This is a sign of family cohesion, a family that is close and whose members communicate with one another. Runaway youth cite poor communication in the family and the desire to have improved communication (Teare, Furst, Peterson, & Authier, 1992). Communication is a skill that is learned and practiced, perhaps through trial and error with peers, parents, or spouses. Some family members have not yet learned how to express their thoughts effectively or to hear what others are *really* saying. A son may say one thing, and his father hears something completely different. For example, son Patrick states, "I would like to have time alone when I come home." When the counselor asks the father what he heard Patrick say, father responds heatedly, "I heard him say that he doesn't want anything to do with me and that I irritate the heck out of him. If he wants to go to his room when he gets home, fine! He can stay there the rest of the night." However, that is not what Patrick said. That is his father's interpretation of Patrick's request. This interpretation is based upon months and maybe years of painful talks and experiences with his son, and the father automatically reacts to his assumptions with anger.

It is always easier to be angry than to be hurt. When you are hurt, you feel vulnerable, but if you are angry, you feel powerful and strong. Unfortunately, anger makes it harder to talk about being hurt (Alexander & Parsons, 1982). After all, it is very hard to hug a porcupine. If this interaction occurred at home between father and son, an argument would likely ensue. They will need assistance to learn how to undo negative communication patterns. Families in pain assume malicious intent in almost anything any other family member might say. Even relatively benign comments with a potentially positive interpretation are doomed to be interpreted as cold-hearted attacks. This is a vicious cycle, but it can be broken.

ABUSE: PHYSICAL, SEXUAL, AND NEGLECT

Many children leave families that pose serious risk to them, including physical and sexual abuse. Studies of runaway and homeless youth have found the incidence of admitted sexual abuse to range from 21 percent and 60 percent (Molnar, Shade, Kral, Booth, & Watters, 1998; Whitbeck, Hoyt, & Ackley, 1997a), and that of physical abuse to range between 16 percent and 40 percent (Molnar et al., 1998; Unger, Kipke, Simon, Montgomery, & Johnson, 1997). Twice as many girls as boys report sexual abuse, whereas males and females report similar levels of physical abuse (Slesnick & Meade, 2001). Between 50 percent and 70 percent of youth report that they were neglected while living in the home (Whitbeck & Hoyt, 1999).

Sexual Abuse

Kids report that the sexual abuse they suffered often was done by boyfriends of their mother or by stepfathers. One youth stated, "All of my mom's boyfriends have forced sex on me. It started when I was 5 and stopped when I left home. I don't talk to my mom anymore. I told her once what one of her boyfriends was doing to me, and she didn't believe me. She got mad and told me I was a lying bitch. She thought I just didn't like him and wanted them to break up. She was real mad." This child reported that her mother was physically abusive to her. She was not alone either; she had nine other siblings, some of whom were also molested. When social services became involved, most of the siblings were separated from one another and put into foster homes. This girl had her first child at age 13 by a man 10 years her senior. She left home to stay with him, but they soon broke up; she went to the streets, and he kept their child.

Several kids report that their parents or foster parents traded them to drug dealers for sex in order for the parents to get drugs. Since this same scenario has been told different times by unrelated children, it appears that it is not uncommon. Perhaps the parent is severely addicted to drugs, has lost contact with reality, and is oblivious of the ramifications of what he is doing. Or worse, perhaps the parent is fully aware of what he is doing and of the effect it has on the child.

As far as society is concerned, an adult who molests a child is at the bottom of the social totem pole. This is evidenced among prisoners who are already poorly valued citizens by many. Child molesters who are put in prison are themselves raped, beaten, and sometimes killed by fellow prisoners.

We know that some child molesters seek out single mothers with young children. These are vulnerable mothers who welcome the offers of help and comfort from a romantic interest. Mothers do not know that these men are molesters; after all, the molesters are not two-headed cyclops with black teeth and club feet. They are normal-looking men with regular jobs and perhaps even social charm.

A child who leaves home for the streets does not always escape from further sexual assault. In fact, street kids post warnings at drop-in centers identifying molesters and rapists. These men often cruise around hangouts for street kids. (The kids are easy targets because they have few advocates and resources.) One molester even asked an older male street kid if he knew any 12- to 13-year-old girls who would party with him. He told the street kid he wanted to take a girl home for his friends to party with, too. Little did this man know of the street youth network. Though street kids may have skirmishes, for the most part they unite against outside threats. They protect their street brothers and sisters.

Therapists and researchers know that treating child molesters is difficult and time intensive. Most do not seek treatment because they do not wish to change. Only when they have been arrested do they go into treatment, and usually only in response to a court order.

Not every child who is raped or molested runs away from home. However, many street kids say that when they tell their mom, she does not believe them. The consequences for telling are sometimes severe. It may include a beating—verbal or physical. It includes disbelief, lack of supportiveness, lack of comfort, or just plain lack of interest. Perhaps the mom cannot even consider the possibility that her daughter was molested because she feels responsible. She might feel that if she keeps telling herself and her daughter that it did not happen, she can make it an absurdity. Some mothers feel threatened and jealous of the attention their daughter gets from the mother's men.

Physical Abuse

Children's reports of physical abuse are no less disturbing. Children report beatings, burns with cigarettes, being locked in closets, and other torture. Many describe conflicts in which weapons are drawn. Imagine a situation where a mother would hold her child under the water in the bathtub as a means of teaching the child a lesson. Or, imagine a father so angry at his son for coming home late that he would throw him against the wall and punch him in the stomach so hard that the child spits up blood. It happens. Some kids fight back when they get older. A 6-year-old is helpless. A 14-year-old is not. A teenager might even throw the first punch or be the first to draw a weapon. A father who is accustomed to having the upper hand in a fight may no longer be able to wield the same power against his son. The son, after all, had an expert instructor in offensive fighting. In fact, the father may state during the police response to domestic violence that his son is "out of control." Sure he is, because the father can no longer control him with violence.

As horrifying as these experiences are, children who suffer serious abuse do not necessarily have futures carved in stone, but that future is at risk. They do not necessarily become abusers in their own families, though the risk is higher. A child who has been abused is also at a much greater risk for being victimized while on his own than a child who has never been victimized in the home (Whitbeck & Hoyt, 1999).

Children learn from their parents to handle problems with violence. However, many learn new ways of dealing with conflict that does not involve violence. A child's first exposure to parenting is through her own parents. Many street kids say they want to help other kids who are like them. They want to be protectors of other children. They want to be better parents than their parents were to them. And many succeed.

Others do not succeed, and do not learn to handle frustration and anger in nonviolent ways. In fact, some of those children, when grown up, are the ones parenting the runaway and street children. Parents who abuse were often abused themselves. Though this is no excuse, they have not put the effort into learning appropriate ways to discipline their own children. Sometimes alcohol and drugs exacerbate poor judgment. Sometimes parents suffer from severe mental illnesses, and this interferes with their ability to parent their children in loving, nonviolent ways. In the end, although we can perhaps understand from the past why parents are violent to their children, responsibility for change lies with them. It does not lie with the child—and nothing a child does deserves a beating.

Neglect

Physical and sexual abuse are overt and easily identified. Neglect as a form of child abuse is less overt but is often as painful. Neglect may include being left alone for 24 hours (or longer) or not having enough food, clothing, or water to drink. Kurtz, Jarvis, and Kurtz (1991) report that homeless youth report parental neglect more often than do nonhomeless youth. These youth have reported that their parents are not available or willing to care for or support them, and that, in essence, they are not wanted by their parents. In one study, 41 percent of youth cited parents' not caring about them as a reason for leaving home (Whitbeck & Simons, 1990).

One case of neglect that child protective services investigated occurred in a family with several runaway teenagers and several young children living in a one-bedroom apartment. The therapist was told that an investigation was currently under way, and that she could still work with the family during the investigation. She would take her own folding chair to the sessions because of the smell of feces and urine on the couches and floor. The mother was severely mentally ill and rocked herself during sessions, almost in a catatonic stupor. A two-year-old ran around the house without a diaper and at one point dropped her lollipop in a puddle on the floor. Horrified, the therapist grabbed the lollipop and rinsed it thoroughly before it was put back into the toddler's mouth. The smell was bad, the filth was bad, and basic needs were not being very well met. The mother never beat the children, and the children were never molested or raped. Yet, all the children, as they reached their early teens, left home for the streets. The children were emotionally close to one another, and while they were on the streets they protected one another. Did they get their basic needs met better on their own than while they lived at home? It is possible that they did.

RELATED YOUTH ISSUES

In understanding why some children leave or are pushed out of the home, some researchers have suggested that children who have trouble early on with their behavior are often those whose parents are least able to cope with them (Whitbeck & Hoyt, 1999). For example, a child may suffer from attention deficit disorder, and at a very young age be very active, always moving, talking, and seeking attention. The child may have trouble focusing on one activity for a long period of time. His mom may be a low-energy woman who has low frustration tolerance. Her forms of recreation are reading, cross-stitching, and watching television. She is not always on the go and does not enjoy physical activity. She has trouble coping with her son's constant energy and demands, and her patience dwindles over time. Eventually, the two are always at odds. The mother is unable to assist her child in slowing down because she gets frustrated and snaps at him during even brief interactions. In time, he snaps back at her for being lazy and inactive.

Researchers suggest that these types of negative interactions between child and parent build upon one another, leading to even more arguments (Patterson & Stouthamer-Loeber, 1984). And more conflict leads to more individual and family problems. When a mother stops her urge to snap at her son and instead responds calmly, the son learns to respond calmly, too.

Usually, a child learns from his parents early that when he gets angry, he needs to handle it in appropriate ways that do not make other people angry. That means he cannot scream, yell, hit, call names, or storm out of the room. A child with problems controlling his behavior, whose parents have trouble helping him control his behavior and who *in addition* may have trouble controlling their own behavior, is a formula for disaster. Aggressiveness in children often leads to rejection by their peers. Most kids do not like mean kids or kids who fly off the handle too quickly. So these aggressive children often drift into groups of other aggressive children (Bahr, Hawks, & Wang, 1993; Dishion, Capaldi, Spracklen, & Li, 1995).

Members of these aggressive youth groups often learn to engage in delinquent behaviors. They may shoplift, experiment with drugs and alcohol, and get into trouble. These kids might get arrested and have poor school performance. Usually, poor school performance is not a result of a lack of intelligence. More likely, they have poor grades because they have difficulty paying attention in class. Many get into fights with other students and are suspended from school. Suspension does not help kids keep up with the class; its puts them farther behind. The child's aggressiveness interferes with her relationship with teachers, too. A teacher is more likely to help a student who is quiet and pays attention in class. A teacher is less likely to help the student who talks back when reprimanded for not paying attention.

These kids often drop out of school. Without school to structure his day and with an unpleasant home to return to, what will the child do with his time? He will spend it with his friends, who are much like him. They do not reject him, and they do not make him feel stupid. In fact, he believes that his friends are the only ones who care about him. They accept him as he is, even with all his faults. He feels that his friends are all that he has in life.

This new-found connection with others is good and bad. On the one hand, it is good because he is connected to other kids and feels a part of a group. Being a part of a larger whole and feeling cared about helps anyone feel good about himself. We feel more worthwhile when others care about us. On the other hand, a group of unsupervised adolescents who have difficulty following rules and controlling their anger can mean trouble. And just as parents model or teach poor ways to handle frustration, peers can model new behaviors. Friends may model cigarette smoking, alcohol or drug use, crime, and street survival. A Norwegian study of schoolchildren indicated that kids who never drank alcohol were characterized by weak ties to peers (few friends), while drinkers were characterized by strong ties to peers (Pedersen & Aas, 1995). In other words, if you are a child with few friends, you are less likely to drink alcohol than if you have lots of friends and feel strongly connected to them. If a street kid (or soon-to-be street kid) wants to be accepted by his friends, he will likely do as his friends do. Otherwise, he risks losing yet another relationship and failing again.

In sum, researchers believe that early behavioral problems in a child, who is born to a parent who cannot effectively deal with these problems, leads to even more serious problems involving school, peers, emotions, or behavior. Alone, a kid can only deal with so much. After all, we are not meant to be alone. Spending all his time with his friends is heaven when compared to going home or going to school. He is tired of going home to angry, frustrated parents, and going to school with teachers and students who do not like him. He is tired of failing his classes. His friends are leaving home, and they invite him to go, and of course he welcomes the opportunity to immerse himself in a new life where at least he has his friends.

PARENT ISSUES

Parental Stress

Several researchers have found that parent problems such as depression, anxiety, and substance use are associated with substance use, depression, and conduct problems among their children (e.g., Burbach & Borduin, 1986; Patterson, 1975; Thomas & Forehand, 1991). Some researchers conclude from their studies that parental stress, including marital problems and conflict, is the root of child problems (Hirsch, Moos, & Reischl, 1985). And in fact, controlled studies have found that homeless adolescents report higher levels of parental marital problems than do adolescents who have never run away from home.

Family systems theorists have long proposed that a child's problems serve a function in the family (Minuchin & Nicols, 1998). That function may be to keep the parents together. By leaving home, the adolescent throws the family into a crisis, which can distract the parents from their own marital or relationship problems. A child's run from home is especially effective at keeping the family together when the parents are nearing separation from one another. Sometimes families do not appreciate that their child is working so hard to keep everyone together. Some kids do more than just run from home. They use drugs, get into trouble at school, and get arrested. Unfortunately, some families *blame* this child (who, remember, is working really hard to save the family) for all of the family's problems. Of course, the child is not thinking to herself, "I'm going to go get in some big trouble now so that I can get my parents to focus on me and not on themselves." And parents don't say to their kids, "Will one of you please distract your mother and me from our fighting so that we can unite to help you." Family members do not realize the impact of their behavior on one another, and when it is pointed out to them, they might respond in disbelief.

When one child stops acting out, therapists may notice that other children in the family begin to rebel. One particularly useful question for parents is, "If all your children were behaving and there were no big problems with any child, what would you and your wife do together?" Focusing away from the children and onto the couple's relationship may be fruitful for jump-starting a positive change process for the entire family.

Parental Mental Health Issues

In addition to parental stress, parental mental health, including depression and substance use, is also related to a child's leaving home. Estimates are that nearly two-thirds of runaway kids' parents have problems with alcohol and 44 percent have problems with hard drugs (Whitbeck & Hoyt, 1999). Parental use of alcohol or drugs is associated with poor parenting skills and greater parental rejection. Substance use in the family also increases the likelihood of physical and sexual abuse of children. In addition to substance use problems among parents, one study reported that 42 percent of youth had at least one parent in trouble with the law (Whitbeck & Hoyt, 1999).

Boundaries

In healthy families, the roles and boundaries between family members are clear. Parents are parents, and kids are kids. Parents are not their child's friend (at least not until they're older and able to self-monitor), and kids are not their parent's parent. Runaway kids may describe one of their parents as their best friend, "We could get high together and party; it was like having my best friend living with me. My mom would hang out with my friends and buy the beer—it was great. She was one of us." Several youth who dealt drugs reported that one or both parents were their best customers. One child's mother was on disability and was a crack cocaine addict. Her live-in boyfriend was also an addict. The money her son made from dealing drugs paid the rent, food, utility, and phone bills. Everyone in the family knew that he was a dealer, and it was appreciated. Fortunately, he did not like dealing, would leave for months at a time to get away from his family, and then would return home. One reason he kept returning home was to check on his younger brother, as he did not want him to end up involved in drugs. This child's therapist got him enrolled in an alternative school after years of truancy. He was doing relatively well until he was arrested and sent to long-term detention for drug trafficking and probation violations.

Parenting Practices

Parenting practices may be especially important in predicting adolescent delinquency. Poor parental monitoring and inconsistent discipline have been identified as key parenting practices related to problems in children (Dishion et al., 1995; Forehand, Miller, Dutra, & Chance, 1997). In one survey, parents of runaway youth viewed themselves as less effective than did parents of nonrunaways (Whitbeck & Hoyt, 1999). Parents of runaways scored themselves significantly lower on measures of parental monitoring than did other parents. These parents were less apt to know where their children were and with whom. They were less likely to establish and enforce a curfew. Interestingly, both homeless youth and their parents reported less effective parenting compared to families of nonrunaways.

SYSTEM ISSUES

The family is not the only vehicle for healthy socialization. In the United States, the nuclear family, composed of a mother, father, and children, is perceived to be the natural organization of humans, while any other structure is labeled pathological. And yet some family situations are so detrimental to the youth's development that the young person is more likely to thrive in an alternative, nontraditional environment. For example, the family may be homeless and unable to meet the basic needs of the children; parents may be addicts; a single-parent mother may be a prostitute and not able to provide a safe and stable environment for her daughter; a father may be violently abusive; or the child may be sexually abused by mother's boyfriends.

System youth generally enter the social services system because of abuse or neglect by primary caregivers. Child Protective Services (CPS) intervenes, and youth are exposed to temporary or permanent out-of-home placements. A large number of children come to the attention of CPS yearly—roughly three million (National Clearinghouse on Child Abuse and Neglect, 2003). Some researchers have noted that children in foster care are often deprived of a sense of belonging and predictability, which may contribute to their continuing maladjustment and problem behavior (Haerian, 1998). Identification of the unique issues among kids who are removed from the home may assist service providers in understanding and addressing problem areas in which these youth are especially vulnerable. With such identification, treatment can then be more effective at intervening in current problems and preventing them from interfering in the child's future.

CONCLUSION

A child leaves home or is asked to leave home because of many different problems that have compounded over time. A child is born into some situations, where the events leading to a runaway episode begin at birth. A poor match of child and parent needs creates fodder for the exacerbation of stress and conflict. Parents already trying to make ends meet, and who have few friends and family members near their home to help them, have trouble devoting the time, and keeping the patience, required to effectively deal with what is on their plate. Much arguing and criticism are characteristic of families with runaway youth. As children take their cues from their parents for how to communicate, it is up to the parents to initiate calm discussions and to change the cycle of negativity.

One event usually does not end up in a runaway episode. Multiple negative events must occur, and they have to occur over and over. Even extremely traumatic events such as physical and sexual assault usually occur multiple times, sometimes over a period of years, before the child leaves the family. In the case of neglect and physical and sexual abuse, the fault clearly lies with the abuser. The child's flight from home can be easily understood in terms of escaping the abuse. In other cases, the fault is not easily identified. The reason a child runs from home is found in many interacting variables, including parent variables (patience, financial resources, mental health problems, stress, social support, their own childhood histories), child variables (personality, friends, access to alternate adult guidance), and the match between child and parent needs and personality. Some children do not run away from home but are removed from the home because of child abuse and neglect, and are thus inducted into the foster care and group home social services system.

A FATHER'S STORY

"All Karen wanted to do was come home, and no one let me bring her back. I abandoned her. All she wanted to do was come home—now she's home," said Paul, her father, choking back tears. Karen was 14 years old. She was found by hospital staff hanging by the neck in her room at a northern California hospital on May 23, 1997. Her arms and legs were covered with bruises from flailing against the wall as she died.

Paul met his wife, Linda, when she ran away from a group home in northern New Mexico. A man picked her up. Sexually abused as a youngster, running away was a part of life for Linda. She had been running away from group homes or hospitals since she was 7 years old. This time she was hitchhiking to Albuquerque and eventually stopped at a race track outside of Albuquerque. Paul, a friend of the man, was at the track that day. Linda was 16 and Paul was 24. They connected and soon married, with Linda's adoptive mother's consent. For a short time, Paul worked for his father, who made and manufactured broccoli rings (the rubber band that holds the broccoli together). After that, he joined the delivery business. Linda was a housewife.

Karen was born to Paul and Linda on their one-year anniversary, February 21, 1983, at University Hospital in Albuquerque, New Mexico. Paul was in the delivery room during the birth. "It was wonderful, the best experience of my life," he recounts. Linda was also thrilled with the birth of Karen. Although she had been a crank addict and an intravenous drug user, she stopped using crank when she discovered she was pregnant. "She only smoked pot and cigarettes when she was pregnant," said Paul. "Although the uterine water was green and the umbilical cord was wrapped twice around the baby's neck, she was in good health," he added.

But the marriage soon ran into trouble. "Linda was cheating on me, and began shooting up drugs and dealing crank again after Karen was born," he said sadly. "When Karen was six months old, I got a call from my mom. Linda had been arrested while trying to sell sex to an undercover cop on a street corner. She had Karen with her. Linda went to jail, and the police took Karen away. My mom went to the police station and brought Karen home." Paul tried to stick it out with Linda, but the cheating, drugs, and prostitution took too much of a toll on the relationship. They divorced in September 1983.

Paul was awarded custody of Karen. Linda could see Karen three days a week at Linda's adoptive mother's home. But Linda rarely appeared during the visiting period, so Paul stopped the visits when Karen was a year old. "Linda could see Karen anytime she wanted," he said. "It ended up being once every three months, and sometimes once every six months. But when Linda was around, she was a good mom. They would do stuff together, she never ignored Karen, and was never mean to her."

The sporadic contact between Linda and Karen lasted a couple of years. When Karen was three years old, Linda had a son. "He could be my son, but we're not sure," said Paul. "When Linda was pregnant, she moved back in with us for two months. Then she left to be with her abusive boyfriend. He once beat her with a two-by-four, so she torched his car. After that, Linda saw Karen only occasionally until Karen was five years old. The car incident as well as the drug dealing and prostitution landed Linda in jail. Karen traveled 200 miles every weekend to see her mother until she was nine years old. In three years, Linda got out on probation, but blew it and was back in jail for another eight months."

When Linda was released from jail, she got a job as a waitress and, for a few months, had lots of contact with Karen. But, in general, Linda was in and out of Karen's life. "Karen was very angry about that," said Paul. She would get comfortable with her mom, and then her mom would leave and she would not hear from her again." All her life, she wanted a family and wanted her mom and dad to work it out.

"I had a girlfriend named Bobbi once. I had been going out with her for six months, and she and Karen were very attached to each other—they were buddies. Karen was going to be four years old, and she and Bobbi were going to plan her fourth birthday party the next day. When Bobbi left, she got in a bad car wreck and died that night. Karen was very upset and at the same time couldn't believe it—'we were supposed to do our fourth birthday,' she had said."

Paul smiled, though it was a sad smile, "Karen was a good kid. She was energetic and eager to grow up. She loved to bowl, having tagged along with me to tournaments. When she was eight years old, she also played softball. She liked that. She was musically inclined and very artistic too. She loved to draw and played the organ. Her friends taught her songs on their keyboard, and also showed her how to play the guitar. We couldn't afford lessons.

"She didn't do very well in school though. She was in special education because of her temper. Teachers and doctors wanted to put her on Ritalin, but she and I refused. In kindergarten, she had fits once in awhile and would get put in time out. She'd get angry. One time, Karen thought a teacher was stealing money because the teacher took money away from one of her friends. Karen belted her. In her opinion, she was right and the teacher was wrong. Karen knew that hitting the teacher was wrong, but the teacher was trying to take money from her two buddies. She was protecting her friends," he said grinning proudly.

Paul continued, "Although Karen was always a jokester, she was angry at home. She was angry at everything. When Karen was three years old, my girlfriend got pregnant, but it wasn't my baby. Karen felt like it was her baby. My girlfriend went back to her other boyfriend, and Karen never got over that. Even seven years later she refused to acknowledge her. I asked her, 'Why are you being that way?' and she said, 'because I know who she is, I can't afford any more heartaches.' She was 10 years old when she said that.

"She loved holidays and was always excited about Halloween, Christmas, Easter, and birthdays. She was happy unless she was throwing a fit about something. She threw a fit when she didn't get her way, and that happened every day."

With a subtly irritated tone, Paul said, "It was hard being a single father because I was always under a microscope. Everyone was watching. Neighbors called the cops on me for beating her and sexually abusing her. She had to get checked by University Hospital to see if she was still a virgin when she was five years old. The police would come out, but in the investigations, I was always cleared. This went on until she was seven years old, then I moved, and the complaints stopped.

"She always had friends everywhere she went, and she always stuck up for the underdog. If she didn't like how other kids treated someone, she would step in. One time, there were two girls in sixth grade that were being threatened by some gang girls, and Karen told them to back off. She had to avoid them for weeks, because I wouldn't let her fight them. And then on the last week of school, she asked me if she could get it over with [fight them]. I told her that she couldn't start it. She didn't. And everyone said the two girls got it worse than Karen did—she only had a couple of bruises," he said, beaming, with tears in his eyes.

When Karen was 10 years old, her mom became involved with heroin and was both dealing and using it. Paul said, "She tried to break away from dealing, but they wouldn't let her. They gave her strychnine, which put her in the hospital for three weeks. That was in April 1994. On May 27, 1994, Linda was taken to Juárez, Mexico and was stabbed 18 times in the front and 18 times in the back. She was stabbed in the throat, too, and that's what killed her. In June, her fingerprints were run in El Paso, and that's how we found out. She was 28 years old."

Paul's voice was shaky but determined, "The police called my mom, and she and the chaplain came to our house to tell me and Karen. Karen was in shock. She was angry when she found out that her mom was dead. But she was angry with her mom before that too, because her mom was always absent from her life. I took it worse, I lost it.... I just lost it. I always loved her." After a long silence, Paul asked for a break and went outside to sit under a tree and smoke a cigarette. After about 10 minutes, he returned to the table.

He continued, "After her mom died, Karen copped an attitude. She was only 11. One night, she was watching television and it was nine P.M., her bedtime. I warned her for two hours that nine P.M. was her bedtime, and she said 'I'm not going to bed!' I said 'Yes you are!' She said, 'No I'm not and you can't make me.' She was in a...kinda like a rocking chair, I went over to pick her up while she was cussing me out and she closed-fisted me on the side of my face. I backhanded her and got her out of that chair, I said, 'You don't say no to anyone.' She said, 'I hate you!' and she sucker punched me on the other side of the head. I backhanded her again. I don't let anyone hit me. She got angry and pulled out a knife in the kitchen. She waved the knife at me, yelling 'I hate you! I hate you!' I said, 'I don't give a fuck what you think of me—get your butt in the car.' I took her to my mom's house so that Karen and I could both get a break. That was the first time I had ever hit her, though sometimes she got it across the butt. I couldn't discipline her, I had to use the voice only.

"In May 1995, Karen went to Oklahoma for a couple of weeks to visit family. From there she flew to California where she went to summer school and lived with my half brother and his wife. She was supposed to come back in August 1995, but she did so well in school that everyone thought it was best that she stay there—except for my dad and Karen. She wanted to come home, and my dad said she should return too.

"I felt something was wrong. My brother was too friendly—too huggy huggy. Karen was hush hush. But he was my brother—you should be able to trust your kid with blood, right? Since we were always under a microscope, if someone touched her, I thought she would tell someone. She told her friend in March 1996 that my brother was molesting her. If she had told me we would have been out of there and back in Albuquerque. I would have beaten him and taken him to jail, and I would have pushed a lot harder for her to come home. She didn't say she was being abused, I suppose because she was a typical teenager—parents are the last to know. Her friend's mother reported the abuse to the state, and Karen was taken away. My brother was arrested. He admitted later that he molested her. He served nine months in jail and got out in June 1997.

"After this happened, her grandpa, my dad, wouldn't allow her over to his house. He believed Karen caused all of the problems, and he disowned her—even though his other son molested her! That devastated her because her grandpa was her idol. When my dad was sick a few months earlier, she sat by his bed at the hospital every day after school until visiting hours were over. She did that for three weeks. So, when he blamed her and cut her off, it just devastated her. My dad wanted me to drop the charges and I wouldn't. I never talked to him after that," Paul paused before he continued.

"In March 1996 she became a ward of the state in California. She told them that if they didn't let her see me that she was going to run away. They told her that she couldn't come back to live with me until she turned 18 years old. They wanted to arrest me for abuse. They thought I was the worst in the world because I didn't know that my daughter was molested. She felt abandoned by everyone. I lost custody of her because I had a screwed-up public defender.

"They let Karen come to Albuquerque in the summer of 1996 for two months. We had a ball. She pleaded with my friends to get me to let her stay—she didn't want to go back. My friends told her to hang in there, and didn't tell me what she had said until after she was gone.

"When she returned to California, she lived with my stepsister whose daughter and Karen were only six months apart and were good friends.

Karen lived there until March 1997. My stepsister turned Karen over to human services because Karen said that my stepsister's husband tried something with her. He denied the whole thing. My stepsister couldn't have the family in an uproar, so Karen was taken out of the home.

"From March 1997 until May 23rd 1997, Karen went to one group home after another. I talked to her at least once week. She started cutting on herself and rebelling even more. She was in and out of the hospital for cutting and suicidal tendencies. She would also tell people that she wanted to kill her uncle.

"The last time I saw Karen was Christmas 1996. I flew out to California for the Rose Parade. It was a good time because we enjoyed each other's company and we were able to talk. There was no fighting and no arguing. She enjoyed it, but she cried because she wanted me to bring her home. I couldn't do that because the state told me that I would be charged with kidnapping if I took her to New Mexico."

At this point, Paul handed me a large stack of hospital admission reports and said, "Everything you need to know from March 1997 until she died is here. I don't want to go through that again." The numerous hospitalization reports and therapy notes state that Karen felt abandoned by all the adults in her life. At times, hospital notes indicated that Karen felt she was not well liked by staff. These statements included, "Patient continues to feed negative feelings onto milieu." Her first hospitalization discharge report stated, "She operated in an angry and entitled manner. She attended group therapy and school when she felt like it. She spoke to adults when she felt like it. She operated as if she was above the rules. Her basic position, while in the hospital, was one of distance, distrust and noncompliance." The report went on to note, "The patient was not able to understand that the individual adults in the hospital treatment team were not her captors. She was angry that her father was not in a position to care for her. She was angry because she felt that she had been the victim of abuse from her father, molestation from her uncle and lack of support from her family, in general, and yet she is being singled out to be hospitalized. She was unable to see that her conduct, both in terms of drug abuse, suicidal ideation [thoughts], and running away from the group home was at all connected with why she was being hospitalized." In hospital notes, Karen complained about having to repeat her story to many different people. And at times, the notes indicated the hospital staff didn't believe Karen. For example, "client reports that her mother was 'murdered,'" with quotation marks to indicate disbelief.

Karen had a suicide pact with three other friends, and prior to her hospitalization, her best friend committed suicide at another hospital. Karen reported that the reason she wanted to die was that her life "sucked." She reported that she had been depressed her whole life, and that she had attempted to kill herself before. She was admitted to the hospital after she cut her arm at the group home with a piece of glass "even after contracting to not harm herself."

Karen was admitted to her first group home on March 24, 1997. She was discharged on April 2, 1997, and hospitalized. Following her discharge on April 16, 1997, she was admitted to another group home, where she was discharged again on April 24 for rehospitalization. She had been on the run from her group home for several days, and was readmitted to the hospital as a danger to self and gravely disabled. This was her second admission to the hospital. After the 30-day stay, she was discharged to another group home on the morning of May 22, 1997. After two hours at the group home, she left, found her way back to the hospital, and was admitted again 10 hours after her discharge. The final discharge report states, "This was the third psychiatric hospitalization for this 14-year-old female who, at the time of hospitalization, had only the hospital as her home. She had cut her legs with a Coke can top and then had engraved the name of her boyfriend into her leg. She told hospital staff that when she got to the group home she felt immediately pressured by them to unpack, make her bed, and follow the home's routine. She said that she did not feel welcomed and that she felt very pressured. She said that she thought she should leave so that she would not harm herself. She called a friend who brought her back to the hospital."

The final discharge report recounts her prior stays at the hospital. "During her most recent hospitalization, Karen had been very difficult to incorporate in the ward's routine. She was oppositional with this writer, the staff and the ward rules. It took her at least two and a half weeks to start to participate in the program. At times, in group therapy, her behavior towards other patients was antagonistic which resulted in her being excused from the group. She maintained a mistrusting and guarded attitude. She had serious problems with attachment and had a very difficult time believing that anybody might be working in her interest. She was easily frustrated. She took issue with anyone doing anything that might compromise her autonomy. Several attempts were made and several solutions were offered for placement for Karen which she refused. She had been placed in two different group homes in the past and had left within a few days stating that she felt suicidal and that people were insensitive to her. Once in the hospital, she denied suicidal ideation or intent."

However, as evidenced by the hospital notes, Karen often reported to hospital staff that life was no good and was at one time observed to repeatedly write, "Fuck this life and everything in it" on a piece of paper while on the ward. In a suicide screen, she told a staff member that she wanted to die and described her ideas of suicide. She told the staff member that she was not afraid of dying and that the sight of her own blood calmed her. That staff member assigned her the highest suicide-risk level. And yet the writer of the final discharge report stated that Karen was not a high risk for suicide—in spite of the multiple cuts on her arms and her stated desire to overdose on pills. The final report notes, "She did not give any staff member, nurse, or therapist any sign that she was contemplating any self-destructive act." It is worth noting that prior to her suicide, Karen told hospital staff, "I don't want to be on this Earth." The report noted that she was to be monitored for safety.

The final paragraph of the last discharge report states, "After group therapy, the patient was to go to physical education. She, as well as several other patients, refused to go. This was not unusual behavior for Karen. As per the ward procedure, she went to her room to rest or read or write letters. At 2:15 P.M., she talked with a staff member on the closed unit for several minutes. Her behavior did not seem out of the ordinary. She was friendly and cooperative. At or around 2:30 P.M. she was observed by the staff member to be sitting on her bed and looking out the window. At around 2:45 P.M., staff heard another patient screaming. They ran to Karen's room and found her hanging from her bathroom door with a bed sheet fashioned as a noose around her neck. She was immediately taken down and given CPR and an emergency medical team was called. She was taken by the emergency team to the emergency room where she was treated and pronounced dead in 30 minutes." Karen did not leave a suicide note. All she wanted was to go home. Now she's home.

Chapter 3

WHO ARE THESE KIDS?

Some researchers argue that running away from home may be a fundamentally healthy reaction to a pathological situation, that life on the streets may be safer than life at home. Running away from home may also represent a poor coping strategy because, in some cases, a bad situation is traded for an even worse situation. Ultimately the question is, who are the kids who leave home? Is the runner more adaptive or less adaptive? Or is he mentally ill? This chapter will review some of the characteristics of youth who leave home. Most of the information is collected from youth after they have already left home. We know less about the child prior to his departure, though we can make educated guesses based upon the retrospective reports of youth. It is clear that youth who turn to the streets have some unique characteristics when compared to the population of nonrunaway youth. However, we cannot know whether these characteristics lead to family troubles and an early departure from home, or if the problems were the result of living on the streets. Overall, relatively little is known about these youth and their families.

AGE

The average age of runaways is 15.8 years (General Accounting Office, 1989). Whitbeck and Hoyt (1999) reported that their sample of Midwestern runaway youth ran away from home for the first time (on average) at age 13.5. They also found that few kids ran away before the age of 10. Thus, it appears that running away, as an option for children, is not used frequently before the onset of the adolescent years. One may surmise that leaving home requires a certain amount of survival skill that in turn, depends upon abstract reasoning skill. These cognitive skills appear in youth during the early adolescent years (Piaget, 1972).

Predictors for determining the age when a child will leave home have not been identified. However, Whitbeck and Hoyt (1999) found that changes in family structure (due to divorce or remarriage) as well as changes in family residence were associated with an earlier age of first running away. Moreover, they found that the younger the child when she first runs away, the more likely she will run again. Our experience in New Mexico is that for some youth, their first runaway episode is so aversive and unpleasant that they never run away again. However, if the negative consequences of running away do not overshadow those of staying in the home, the chances of future runaway episodes increase. Although it may be hard to imagine a 14-year-old choosing to live on the streets rather than at home, even young children have the urge to escape from pain and to survive. Young children age quickly living on the streets. They learn to find food and shelter and to fend for themselves, even though they cannot legally work or sign a lease and do not have access to institutional support such as welfare or food stamps. A 14-year-old on the streets is faced with adult problems, but with fewer resources. Consequently, around survival issues, these youth are very precocious.

ETHNICITY

Although running away from home presents a family crisis regardless of ethnicity, a greater understanding of the areas of risk associated with ethnicity should be examined so that culturally appropriate intervention measures may be tailored to the specific needs of families. In the runaway literature, it is interesting to note that many studies report large samples of minority youth, although analyses examining ethnic differences on the studies' various dependent measures were not conducted.

In New Mexico, the recent census report estimates the population as 50 percent Anglo, 37.5 percent Hispanic, 7.2 percent Native American, 1.8 percent African American, and .8 percent "other." Among adolescents residing in an Albuquerque runaway shelter, 37 percent identify their ethnicity as Anglo, 47 percent Hispanic, 8 percent Native American, 5 percent African American, .6 percent Asian, and 3.1 percent "other." The youth shelter population roughly mirrors the census report of ethnic and racial distribution. We may conclude, then, that running away from home crosses ethnic and racial groups. Factors such as family interactional patterns, family support, family stress, and so on likely play a much stronger role in understanding why youth run away from home than does ethnicity or race.

Our New Mexican sample of street youth shows a similar ethnic and racial composition of shelter-residing youth, but with a higher proportion of Anglo youth: 56 percent Anglo, 34 percent Hispanic, 5 percent Native American, and 5 percent "other." Shelter-residing youth are primarily those who have families living in the area, whereas street youth are more transient, passing through New Mexico from all over the country. This influx of street youth from other parts of the country may partially account for the higher proportion of Anglo youth that we see.

Recently, Slesnick, Vasquez, and Bittinger (2002) examined family-relatedness problem behaviors in Hispanic and Anglo runaway youth between the ages of 12 and 17. Although reports of level of family conflict did not differ, the means of resolving conflict did. Hispanic youth reported that they used less hitting, slapping, name calling, storming out, and the like to resolve disagreements with their parents than did Anglo youth. Given that Hispanic youth also showed greater familistic attitudes of strong attachment, loyalty, and commitment to nuclear and extended family, it follows that they would be more likely to resolve conflict using less-aggressive conflict resolution measures. Overall, Hispanic runaway youth reported more depression and less acting out than did Anglo runaway youth. Possibly, Hispanic parents work harder than Anglo parents to set boundaries and limits using stricter and firmer parenting measures, utilizing whatever means are necessary to prevent acting-out behaviors.

GENDER

Few studies have examined gender differences among runaway youth. National survey data report equal numbers of males and females among runaway and street youth. In our sample of New Mexican youth, we find that among street youth, 58 percent are male. Among shelter-residing youth, 60 percent are female. In sum, both local and national data show that gender does not differentiate youth who are told to leave or voluntarily run away from home. Even so, factors leading up to a child's departure from home may be influenced by gender. Although researchers have not yet identified predictors, or factors that lead to running away from home, we know that these youth have more troubled family environments than those who do not leave home. And we have some information that, prior to leaving home, males and females experience different family-related traumas.

In the area of physical and sexual abuse, gender differences among runaway and homeless youth are pronounced. Some researchers have found that more female, compared to male, runaways report having experienced sexual abuse while in their homes, and more males report physical abuse. For example, Molnar et al. (1998) found that females were more likely to report sexual (70%) than physical (35%) abuse, while males were more likely to report physical (35%) rather than sexual (24%) abuse. Similar to the above-cited research, 48 percent of the females in our program report sexual abuse, and 50 percent report having experienced physical abuse. Among males, 15 percent reported sexual abuse, while 50 percent reported physical abuse. An equal proportion of males and females reported having been hit, slapped, punched, or had a weapon used on them by a household member. Yet, similar to national data, females are more likely to report having been sexually abused. As an aside, males may be more likely than females to underreport sexual abuse because of shame or pride. This is not to say that females do not feel shame or pride, but our society allows for, and is more comfortable with, the expression of feelings related to rape and sexual abuse among females than among males.

Gender Differences While on the Streets

Whitbeck and Hoyt (1999) found that in their sample of Midwestern street youth, males were 1.5 times more likely to spend time on the streets than females. Possibly, males are able to physically defend themselves better than are females. Females may be greater targets for sexual assault while on the streets, and they may remove themselves from physically living on the street more quickly than males. In fact, the rate of sexual assault on homeless women is reported to be approximately 20 times the rate among women in general (Kelly, 1985). Many girls report hooking up with male counterparts for protection while on the streets, and may be able to move into hotels or crash in another youth's apartment. Thus, though homeless girls may be less likely to sleep in doorways, in parks, or on rooftops, they still live in unstable, homeless situations.

Substance Use

In the substance abuse treatment literature, 75 percent of clients who receive services for substance use disorders are male. Yet, among runaways, the gender difference disappears so that equal proportions of males and females meet criteria for the diagnosis of substance abuse disorders (Kipke, Montgomery, Simon, & Iverson, 1997). Again, one can speculate that, when living on the streets, the use of alcohol and/or drugs is an accepted, and perhaps even an encouraged, cultural behavior that transcends gender. The desire to escape from emotional pain is universal, and while on the streets, few tools are available to facilitate this escape. We know that drugs are readily available to youth on the streets, and alternative means of coping are not. Whether youth who leave home had problems with substance abuse prior to their departure is not known. We can assume that youth's substance use becomes exacerbated while living on the streets.

Emotional Problems

In the general population, females report more internalizing problems such as depression or anxiety, while males report more externalizing problems such as violence and legal problems. These internalizing patterns also show up among runaway youth. In a survey of 775 street and shelter youth between the ages of 12 and 19 (Molnar et al., 1998), more females (48%) had attempted suicide than males (27%). Our New Mexico program also shows significantly more female youth diagnosed with major depression and panic disorder (anxiety) than male youth. However, we do not see a difference between male and female runaways in externalizing problem behaviors. Females and males report no difference in violent, delinquent, or aggressive behaviors.

Violence

We have some evidence that runaway and homeless boys may underreport their violent activities, while girls are more likely to provide an accurate picture of their violent and aggressive transgressions. For example, we find that boys deny gang affiliation on our assessment instruments. However, boys will report active, frequent involvement in gang fighting during a later point in the interview process. Females report both gang affiliation and gang fighting, with a significant and positive correlation between the two. Several possible explanations may be entertained for this finding. In the juvenile justice or public school system, males have reported punitive treatment from staff if they are identified as gang members. A boy who has honed his survival skills learns quickly what he needs to do to protect himself against maltreatment, which means keeping his gang affiliation to himself.

In addition, our data show that although females and males report similar levels of illegal, delinquent behaviors, males report three times more arrests. Thus, though behaviors might be similar between males and females, females may not suffer as severe consequences by police or institutional staff for their misbehaviors. Females might still benefit from the perception that males—not females—are the violent ones. Female street youth may be given greater benefit of the doubt and sympathy by police and others, and may be less frequently detained.

VIOLENCE AND DELINQUENCY

Regardless of gender, runaway and homeless youth are more violent than their nonrunaway peers. This is likely because they have to use force to respond to desperate situations while living on the streets. For example, if the child is a drug dealer and gets cheated, responding with verbal reasoning skills to the drug-addicted buyer (who has a short attention span) is less effective than throwing the buyer against the wall. Also, a hungry homeless girl may strong-arm a woman for her purse in order to fend off the feeling of imminent death from starvation, even though prior to leaving home for the streets, she volunteered at a hospital on the children's cancer ward.

Investigators theorize that criminal behavior by runaway and homeless adolescents is due to the experience of being homeless, and not to predisposing family and personal variables (Hagan & McCarthy, 1992; McCarthy & Hagan, 1992). These authors suggest that hunger and lack of shelter lead to theft, and unemployment leads to prostitution. Similarly, Baron and Hartnagel (1998) found that the street subculture increases an adolescent's risk of becoming involved in violence on the streets. While both studies acknowledge the background and developmental variables associated with delinquency in street youth (family violence, poverty, and social support), each emphasizes the situational factors related to homelessness as primary contributors to the runaway youth's choice to commit violent and delinquent acts.

One situational factor associated with street living is substance use. Several studies indicate that youth who report persistent substance abuse also engage in delinquency, including committing violent and delinquent acts. Acknowledging this elevated level of substance use in runaway youth, and in an effort to understand violent delinquency among these adolescents, Baron and Hartnagel (1998) investigated drug and alcohol use as predictors of violent criminal acts among a sample of runaway adolescents. They found that alcohol use predicted simple assaults, but illicit drug use did not. Specifically, respondents in their study reported that they were more likely to engage in physical fights under the influence of alcohol.

It is equally plausible that runaway and homeless youth are more violent because they were victimized in violent ways by their parents or siblings. This view is also supported by studies showing that violent, delinquent behavior in adolescents is correlated with victimization by family members or peers (Famularo, Kinscherff, Fenton, & Bolduc, 1990). Parents model violent behaviors to their children, who learn to interact violently with others (Elliott, 1994; Fagan, Piper, & Moore, 1986).

When one combines a history of violent victimization with a street subculture that commands violence and criminality for survival, the likely result is a violent kid. We may not be able to conclude that the child was violent prior to going to the streets, but it is not a far leap to assume that those youth who were victimized while in their homes developed a predisposition to violence.

GAY AND LESBIAN YOUTH

Many gay and lesbian youth are rejected by their families and forced to leave home (Kruks, 1991). Usually, it is because the parents are unable to tolerate their child's sexual orientation. Some parents consider homosexuality a sin that is punishable in the afterlife. These parents believe so strongly that their child is going down the wrong life path that they remove the child from their home.

High rates of attempted suicide, depression, and substance use have been documented among gay, lesbian, and bisexual (GLB) youth (Safren & Heimberg, 1999; Savin-Williams, 1994). However, few researchers have addressed ways to change patterns of dysfunction among GLB youth. Sullivan (1994) noted that "conservatives in Congress abhor any acknowledgement of gay and lesbian minors and seek to expunge all references to this group as a population in need of special services" (p. 291). Sullivan asserted that GLB youth face unique developmental challenges and that service providers should examine the systemic obstacles to competent services in their behalf. Although the lesbian and gay community has improved the legal standing of gays and lesbians in the last 20 years, homosexuality is still illegal in 26 states, and hate crimes are on the increase (Kruks, 1991). Because of the stigma and fear of being identified as gay, youth in general are very reluctant to self-identify as gay.

GLB Youth on the Streets

In New York, estimates are that as many as one-half of youth on the streets are gay or lesbian (Humm, 1990), while 40 percent of the homeless youths in Seattle are estimated to be gay (Seattle Department of Human Resources, 1988). Although, as noted earlier, most studies identify roughly equal numbers of male and female homeless youth, lesbian youth are less often identified than gay male youth (Kruks, 1991). In the general adolescent population of 29 million, 3 million are either gay or lesbian, with 35 percent being males under age 19, and 6 percent to 11 percent being female (Centers for Disease Control, 1993; Herdt, 1989; James, 1978). In his sample of homeless gay youth at a Los Angeles Community Services Center, Kruks (1991) reported that 79 percent were male and 21 percent were female.

There are several differences between gay street youth and their nongay counterparts. Gay street youths share many of the problems that other street youth have, but also have to face an additional set of problems stemming from the rejection and low self-esteem experienced because of their sexual orientation. Although most studies examining street youth do not focus on gay street youth, some studies included these youth in their sample. Several studies found that gay street youth attempt suicide at three to six times the rate of their nongay homeless peers (e.g., Kruks, 1991; Schneider, Farberow, & Kruks, 1989). Among those GLB youth who had attempted suicide, 53 percent had attempted suicide at least once, and 47 percent more than once (Schneider, Farberow, & Kruks, 1989).

In our work with street youth, more youth identify themselves as bisexual (28%) than as either gay or lesbian (5%). Also, many youth engage in same-gender sex, but do not identify themselves as gay, lesbian, or bisexual. We hypothesized that these youth are more open to love in any form it may present itself than are nonhomeless youth. Homeless individuals anecdotally describe life on the streets as lonely. Youth who suffer abandonment and great interpersonal loss are particularly hungry for affectionate contact, regardless of how it is presented. Youth have stated in response to questions about their sexuality, "I don't care if it's a guy or a girl, I only care about who the person is."

Though we find that the gender and racial/ethnic proportion of runaway and homeless youth roughly matches the general population, GLB youth are disproportionately represented on the streets. As noted, this may be due to greater parental rejection. It is also possible that their struggle for adjustment interacts with their lives at home to make them especially vulnerable for leaving home prematurely.

MENTAL HEALTH ISSUES

We know that runaway and homeless youth have higher rates of mental illness than youth who are living in stable environments. We do not know if the mental illness arose after the child left home, or if it was present prior to the child's departure. However, if there were no definite signs of mental illness while the child was in the home, certainly the stage was being set for problems. Before a child leaves home, there usually is a significant amount of stress or trauma. Long-term abuse or conflict takes its toll on even the most emotionally resourceful people. Thus, these children, if not reporting psychological problems while in the home, likely developed a predisposition toward a clinical disorder that surfaced while trying to survive the streets.

After Leaving Home

Shelter-dwelling runaway youth report that their greatest needs concern living arrangements, family relationships, and communication with their parents (Post & McCoard, 1994). Teare et al. (1992) found that, in their sample of shelter youths, those not reunified with their families had higher levels of hopelessness and suicide ideation than those who were reunified. Those youth not reunified were at greater risk of suicide, had more overall dissatisfaction with life, and had more generalized negative expectations about the future.

One might ask, "If these kids left home to get away from their parents, why do they miss their parents? Why are they suicidal?" At a shelter for abused children, one five-year-old girl who was sexually abused by her parents, routinely locked in a closet for hours, and had cigarette burn marks on her face and arms often cried at night for her mother. Runaway and homeless kids are not much different. These kids always hope that their parents will change and will love them the way that love is supposed to be expressed. Perhaps human nature does not allow us to easily let go of our parents and the desire for their love. After all, everyone strives to experience unconditional love.

Several studies report high rates of mental illness among homeless youth (Schweitzer & Hier, 1993; Unger et al., 1997). Mundy et al. (1990) found that 29 percent of their sample of homeless youth reported experiencing four or more psychotic symptoms on a psychotic symptom index. Our study has found that 75 percent of youth meet criteria for one or more clinical diagnoses other than substance abuse or dependence. The most common reported diagnoses include conduct and oppositional defiant disorder, major depression, obsessive-compulsive disorder, and post-traumatic stress disorder.

Not surprisingly, since these kids have many things to be sad about (for example, lack of a relationship with parents and current living conditions), studies note that the rate of clinical depression among runaway and homeless youth ranges from 29 percent to 83.6 percent (Unger et al., 1997; Yates, MacKenzie, Pennbridge, & Cohen, 1988). One behavior for which street youth are at particular risk is suicide attempts. Studies indicate that from 33 percent to 50 percent of these youth have attempted suicide (Ringwalt, Greene, & Robertson, 1998; Sibthorpe, Drinkwater, Gardner, & Bammer, 1995; Yoder, 1999), compared to the 2 percent to 13 percent of youth in general who have done so (Earls, 1989; Smith & Crawford, 1986).

HIV PREVALENCE AND HIGH-RISK BEHAVIORS WHILE ON THE STREETS

When a youth leaves home for the streets, his risk of HIV infection increases. The unpublished recommendation of a 1989 Public Health Service Consensus Conference on HIV Prevention Strategies for Homeless and Runaway Youth included the prediction that these street youth will become part of the third wave of the HIV epidemic (Sherman, 1992). The extent to which homeless adolescents nationally have already become infected with HIV is unknown, but reported figures from cities around the country are disturbing. Rates range from 6 percent to 12 percent in San Francisco (Daley, 1988; Shalwitz, Goulart, Dunnigan, & Flannery, 1990) to 5 percent in New York (Stricof, Kennedy, Nattell, Weisfuse, & Novick, 1991).

Infection correlates with time on the streets: The longer a young person has been homeless, the more likely he or she is to be infected. Gould (1993) suggests that, "In major cities, like New York, Washington and Miami, infection in teenage runaways is close to 10 percent" (p. 36), compared to a national average of 3 percent among adults and adolescents over the age of 13. Moreover, a study of a small sample of New York City adolescent prostitutes showed that 22 percent tested positive for HIV (Wallace & Weiner, 1994). The markedly higher HIV rates among runaway and homeless youth relative to other adolescent populations supports the assertion that HIV prevention programs for this population are an important public health priority (Rotheram-Borus et al., 1994). However, little evaluation research is available to guide program developers regarding the content, timing, or format for HIV risk reduction interventions targeting teenagers (St. Lawrence, 1993).

High-Risk Drug-Use Behaviors

Homeless youth are especially at risk for HIV given their high level of IV drug use and sexual risk behaviors. The use of IV drugs such as heroin and injectable cocaine increases the direct transmission of the HIV virus through the sharing of drug-injecting equipment. Pennbridge, Freese, & MacKenzie (1992) found that, of those who had engaged in IV drug use within the previous 30 days, 34 percent reported sharing needles. Although alcohol and noninjection drug use are not directly linked to HIV infection, the use of drugs and alcohol can greatly influence adolescents' sexual HIV risk behaviors.

High-Risk Sexual Behaviors

Sexual activity of runaway youth may be categorized in three ways— rape, survival sex, or relationship sex—reflecting the degree of personal control (Athey, 1995). Although the frequency of rape among homeless girls is not known, 25 percent in a New York City shelter stated that they had been raped at some time in their lives (Shaffer & Caton, 1984). Less information is available on rape of young boys, but street workers report it as not infrequent (Able-Peterson, 1989). Rapists are considered to be high-risk carriers for HIV owing to the large number of persons with whom they have sexual contact.

In order to survive, runaways tend to drift quickly into prostitution and pornography to get money for a meal or drugs or shelter. Reports of survival sex or prostitution have varied dramatically (Hollywood, 30%; Los Angeles, 28%; New York City, 3%). It is estimated that there are 900,000 adolescent prostitutes in the United States, and a sample of Seattle adolescent prostitutes reported that condoms were rarely used (Deisher, Farrow, Hope, & Litchfield, 1989).

Moreover, researchers have found that, as the frequency of substance use increases in homeless youth, the number of sexual partners increases and condom use decreases. The significant relationship of substance use to sexual risk behaviors is particularly alarming due to the magnitude of substance use among homeless youth, as noted earlier. In a sample of New York City runaways, 47 percent of males and 16 percent of females reported having 10 or more opposite-sex partners (Rotheram-Borus et al.,

1992), and 98 percent of male street youth in Los Angeles had multiple partners (Pennbridge et al., 1992). These findings are dramatic when compared to 7 percent of a national sample of older male adolescents having 11 or more sex partners and 5 percent of female adolescents having 10 or more sex partners (Miller, Turner, & Moses, 1990).

Street kids who engage in prostitution or survival sex often maintain a heterosexual or homosexual relationship (Athey, 1990). For some couples, one person may engage in prostitution as a mutual decision between the couple, when they are not able to survive through other means. In these couples, often one member serves as the protector who watches out for the partner. The protector might meet the partner after a trick and walk or drive the partner to different spots. In talking to these kids, prostitution is for them just a job. They have set prices, which may vary depending upon how well the john is dressed. None say they like this job, but all say they have to work in order to survive.

Most of the sexual activity of homeless adolescents is unsafe sex, without the use of condoms. Rotheram-Borus, Koopman, & Bradley (1989) found that, in a sample of New York City youth, only 40 percent who were sexually active had ever used a condom, and none had always used one during sexual intercourse. The lack of contraception is also evidenced by high pregnancy rates in homeless girls. A study of health care services to the homeless in 19 cities found that of all 16- to 19-year-old homeless girls seen by the health care projects, 31 percent were pregnant, a rate described by researchers in the project as "astonishing." Another survey found that more than half of the sample of female runaways had been pregnant at least once (Anderson, Freese, & Pennbridge, 1994). In fact, when you consider that this compares to 9 percent of 16- to 19-year-old girls in a non-runaway sample (Wright, 1989), it truly is astonishing.

Childhood Sexual Abuse

Runaway and homeless youth with a history of sexual abuse prior to leaving home may be at greater risk for HIV infection while living on the streets than those youth who were not abused. That is, researchers and clinicians have identified a connection between unresolved childhood sexual trauma and the abuse survivor's increased risk for HIV infection. Carmen and Rieker (1989) initially alerted mental health professionals to this connection through an anecdotal case study report. These authors paralleled the abuse survivor characteristics of sexual compulsivity and revictimization with impulsive high-risk sexual behaviors.

Why would a history of sexual abuse increase one's chances for HIV infection? It appears that youth with a history of abuse engage in more high-risk, potentially suicidal behaviors. Although more research has examined the association between childhood sexual abuse and HIV among adults, several studies have noted this relationship among adolescents. Among youth aged 13 to 18, a history of physical abuse, sexual abuse, or rape was related to a variety of HIV risk behaviors, including IV drug use, prostitution, and more unprotected sex compared to nonabused youth (Cunningham, Stiffman, & Dore, 1994). And, these deleterious effects of abuse increased over time.

Another explanation for this connection is that sexually abused adolescent runaways focus primarily on present survival over any major concerns for the future (Kaliski, Rubinson, Lawrence, & Levy, 1990). Kaliski et al. (1990) noted that these runaway abuse survivors commonly experience chronic depression and believe that they would die if they got AIDS, and that would put an end to their worry and struggle.

SUBSTANCE ABUSE

Though evidence is overwhelming that substance abuse among runaway and homeless teens overshadows that of nonhomeless teens, we cannot know if youth engage in high levels of substance use prior to leaving home or if leaving home leads to heavy substance use. More likely and similar to the discussion on mental illness and violence, the event of leaving home serves to exacerbate weaknesses or other presenting problems that the youth may already have—including alcohol or drug use. However, further research in the form of long-term longitudinal studies are needed to tease apart these relationships. Longitudinal studies follow a sample of youth, who have not run away from home, for several years. With such a design, the relative contribution of several factors expected to predict running away and related problem behaviors can be evaluated, as well as consequences of running away from home.

Theories abound regarding the etiology of substance abuse. Perhaps learning, family history, coping, emotion regulation, genetic predisposition, and cognitive deficits are all at play. Goodman (1972) identified two dominant personal determinants for substance use: psychic pain and inability to cope. He suggested that some degree of psychic pain with which the individual is unable to cope may trigger abusive substance use. Indeed Myers, Brown, and Mott (1993) identified coping as a significant predictor of substance use and relapse. Runaway and homeless youth often face a great deal of psychic pain and difficult situations. These situations include premature independence from their families of origin and traumatic childhood experiences, including physical and sexual abuse and abandonment by loved ones.

Although we do not have information about children's substance use prior to their departure from home, street surveys provide some information about the types of drugs used and the frequency of substance use among homeless youth.

Drug Use on the Streets

The substance abuse rate of homeless youths is estimated to range from 70 percent to 95 percent (Booth & Zhang, 1997; Rotheram-Borus et al., 1989). In comparing a New York City sample of runaways to adolescents in general, Koopman, Rosario, and Rotheram-Borus (1994) report that runaways are three times more likely to use marijuana, seven times more likely to use crack and cocaine, five times more likely to use hallucinogens, and four times more likely to use heroin. Four California studies found that between 30 percent and 40 percent of runaways had used intravenous (IV) drugs (Anderson et al., 1994; Kral, Molnar, Booth, & Watters, 1997; Pennbridge et al., 1992; Yates et al., 1988); markedly lower prevalence rates were identified in New York City, where between 0.3 and 5 percent of runaway and homeless youth reported IV drug use (Koopman et al., 1994; Rotheram-Borus et al., 1989, 1991; Shaffer & Caton, 1984). In our sample of runaway youth, IV drug use is not uncommon; 16 percent of the kids between the ages of 12 and 17 report IV drug use behavior. IV drug using youth who work to clean themselves up and apply for jobs have to wear long-sleeved shirts to cover their abscessed veins and tracks from potential employers. Many of these kids are ashamed of the scars and tell stories of their desperate addiction with sadness and dismay.

Alcohol

Alcohol abuse among street youth is not uncommon. In their sample of runaway youth, Smart and Adlaf (1991) found that almost 50 percent reported current alcohol problems at a clinically significant level, and 9 percent drank alcohol daily. Similarly, two additional studies found that nearly 50 percent of their respective samples of runaway youth met criteria for a diagnosis of alcohol abuse, which is six to eight times higher than among nonrunaway peers. As street youth leave home early and face many adult struggles before they should have to, they also use alcohol at younger ages and experience more problems associated with alcohol use compared to nonhomeless adolescents (Kipke, Montgomery, & MacKenzie, 1993). Some of these problems include alcohol-related arrests, violence, and alcohol poisoning, as well as attempted suicide, involvement in survival sex or prostitution, and length of time homeless. Adolescent alcohol users suffer physical symptoms that over time can lead to chronic liver damage. Heavy alcohol use is also associated with a general pattern of poor diet and stunted growth.

DAVID'S STORY: THE DEALER

I met David at the youth drop-in center. He was waiting for me in front of the building, talking and laughing with another youth. I walked up to him and introduced myself. When I held out my hand, he grasped it firmly and gave me a big grin. As we headed for my car, he hoisted a large, black duffel bag containing all of his belongings over his shoulder. He glanced at me as we talked, sizing me up. David was handsome and young looking; his eyes were bright blue, his hair was blonde, and he looked to be physically fit. He wore blue jeans and a white T-shirt with a blue denim jacket—the pants were dusty and the shoes were old. When he smiled, his teeth looked like they had taken a beating—just like the teeth of a youth who lacked daily access to a toothbrush. This was a man who had grown up on the streets.

There were no awkward silences in the drive to my office. David talked easily and fast. This is David's story as he tells it.

"I was born December 29, 1981, in Albuquerque at 8:01 P.M. My dad was rough, verbally, but was not physically abusive. He would wash my mouth out with soap and spanked me with belts. He never hit me, just belted me. After a few years I said to him, 'Come on! Give me more!' But he was a good guy. He always provided for me. He was one of those redneck Georgia boys, a real racist. I'm not racist though, I'm the only white boy in my gang. I hate racists.

"My mom is the greatest woman in the world. She always tried to keep me out of trouble. She always tried to keep me in her grasp; she did not want me on the streets, getting into trouble. When I got older, she learned I was a lost cause and gave up.

"Both my mom and dad were married before. They each had two kids from their other marriages. I was the only one they had together. My dad had a vasectomy, and I was always teased that I wasn't really his son. They were married to each other for 11 years, and he died of lung cancer. I was 6 when he died, but I remember it. He was pronounced dead at 1:03 A.M. on Wednesday, April 8. My mom came to my room and told me that dad was dead. I didn't care. But I got up and touched his cold hand. The last thing I said to him before he died was 'Fuck off, go to hell' because he wanted me to go to bed and I wanted to watch a movie. I wish he was still around.

"My dad was a long-haul truck driver for 23 years and taught truck driving at the community college. When I was two years old, he stopped driving because he got lung cancer. Besides smoking cigarettes, earlier in life he did pot and acid. He was an alcoholic, but my mom gave him an ultimatum when I was first born, and he stopped drinking. I never saw him drunk. He was a Vietnam veteran too; he was a good man.

"My mom always worked. We weren't poor—she made over $100K. She was an underwriter and now she's the vice president of a bank. I was always very well taken care of.

"When I was born, my older half brother lived with us, but he was involved in drugs and went into the Navy. Now he's a Southern Baptist and a teacher in South Carolina. My other brother was in and out of the penitentiary all of his life. He was a hard-core addict, and had been doing drugs most of his life—that's how I got started on pot and speed. He never ran away from home—he was better to my mom than I was. But he did a lot more drugs than me. He's 29 years old, and was released from the pen to a six-month rehabilitation program where he's doing really well. He's sober now. I'm really proud of him.

"He beat me real bad when I was 12 years old. That's the only time I was ever abused. He beat me up so bad, though, that the state threatened to take me away from my mom for her failure to protect. How could my mom protect me against him? He's 6´3´´ and it took three guys to get him off of me. The police came and were going to take me away, but I told them that the only way they'd take me out of there would be in a body bag. So they left me. Since then we never fought like that again. We love each other. We always loved each other, and he has almost always been there for me. My other half brother and sister never lived with me, so I'm not real close to them.

"In elementary school I broke windows, threw rocks, hit people. I always had a temper, and when my dad died I was a time bomb waiting to happen. When he died, things changed. Before he died, I never used drugs, and I was more sneaky because I was scared of him. He had control over me. He'd yell at me and say, 'you pansy stop whining.' You know, he'd chew me out when I did shit wrong. He was verbally abusive, but I didn't know different. My mom would tell him to watch his mouth. Really, my dad was a great guy. He never physically abused me, only belted me.

"I remember that I used to read him articles out of *Highlight* magazine when he was dying. I would give anything to have him back. When he died, my mom was devastated, and she has never remarried. She says, 'I divorced one and buried one, that's enough.' She won't even date.

"When my dad died, her and my relationship changed. She was treated for ulcers, but it was because of me. I became a little devil and a little shit. She couldn't discipline me; she tried to spank me, and I just laughed at her. If she tried to put me in my room, I would just go out my window. I always did the exact opposite of whatever she wanted me to do. In her shoes, I would have killed me because of what I did to her. Really, I mean it....I would have killed me if I were her. I stole over $40,000 from her over my life. She did the best she could; it wasn't her fault. She still gives me money when I need it, even though I took so much from her.

"I started using pot when I was 6 years old. I started smoking cigarettes when I was 6 years old too, and my dad caught me. He didn't even spank me...like he didn't really care that I was smoking. He just lectured me and made me smoke the rest of the pack right there. When I was 10 years old I started using methamphetamines, and when I was 15 I started with hallucinogens. I've been drinking since I can remember. Every Christmas I'd take shots and drink other people's drinks when they weren't looking.

"Because I was acting out really bad and using a lot of drugs, when I was 12 years old I went to the university's Children's Psychiatric Hospital [CPH]. I got out four months later and went back to middle school. I did good for about two weeks after I got out, but nothing went into my head.

"Three months later I went back into CPH because I was getting worse. I was seeing a counselor at the university, and at our session he said, 'Let's go for a walk.' So we were walking, and when we got close to CPH, a bunch of university security guards slammed me to the ground and I got hospitalized again. Seriously! There was a whole bunch of university security guards, and I was a lot smaller then than I am now—I was not over 100 pounds. At the time, I blamed it all on my mom, but it wasn't her fault.

"That time I was at CPH for one and a half years, and then I was transferred to another residential treatment center for another one and a half years. I was in the hospital for three years total, and I didn't get out until I was 15 years old. I was there so long because I never got better. When I got out, I was transitioned into the high school in our neighborhod and went to day treatment.

"I started smoking weed the first day I got out, but I never went back to rehabilitation. The next place I showed up was jail. I was in and out of trouble, but nothing real big. I mostly did what my mom asked me to do. I was nothing compared to what I was before I went into the hospitals, because I didn't want to go back.

"The trouble I'm in now is the biggest I have had to deal with. I'm not scared though. I want to straighten up, but I can't until I deal with this. Last week I was arrested for trafficking crack cocaine, conspiracy to commit murder, and assaulting a police officer. It was a deal that went bad. I think I'm going to have to do time.

"The first time that I went to the streets was when I was 11 years old. I left because I wanted to get away from my mom. I wanted my freedom. I didn't want to have to answer to nobody. She wanted me to clean my room, go to school, anything that a normal decent boy should do. She never asked much of me—I just didn't want to listen.

"The first time I left, I went to the park and stayed there for a week. The second time, also when I was 11, I left for months. I just did it [ran away] whenever I felt like it. She called the cops to keep an eye out for me; she called her friends and family. She sent my brother to look for me. But, I was nowhere to be seen—that's why they call me Ghost.

"I'm cocky; there's no shame to my name. I sleep in parks, break into houses that are for sale, sleep in backyards and with friends when they have their own place. And yes, I get hungry. And yes, I go through dumpsters for food. I ran away over 20 times between the ages of 11 and 18. By the time I was 18 years old, I wanted to stay at my mom's house.

"After high school, I had too much time on my hands. I screwed up at every job I had. I'd get into trouble, quit, or get fired. With all of the free time, I'd get bored and punch holes in the wall or windows. Boredom got me into trouble. It really got me in trouble. I started breaking into houses, and when I turned 19 I got worse.

"My mom kicked me out of her house every year that I lived with her. I don't hold a grudge about that. I will never live in her house again. When I lived with her last year, the night before my birthday, I took her credit card. I was at a bar, and I went to an ATM and took out $15,000 over about two days. She won't ever let me live with her again. She has a restraining order on me now, so I'm not allowed near her property. But she will still give me my stuff that I have stored there if I need it. Or, she'll give me money if I need it—but I don't like to ask her. She doesn't like to give me money either. But she loves me and won't deny me when I'm in dire need. Without my friends or family I'd be dead. They've helped me in situations where I'd be killed—like I owed money and all other sorts of situations.

"I've never had my own apartment for more than one and a half months. I've stayed in six different ones. That's because I sell drugs—I know how to hustle without getting caught. I've been arrested four times as an adult and six times as a minor. When I was a minor, the police took me to the detention home just to scare me. They always took me home and never actually put me in the detention home overnight because I was really young. The first time that I was handcuffed and put in the back of the police car was when I was nine years old. I took a $100 chemistry set from a store, I just walked out with it. After the police took me home, my mom grounded me and put me in my room for two and a half days.

"I have nothing to hide; there's no shame to my game. When I was 6 years old, I was caught with a gun at my elementary school. I stole it from a neighbor's house. I tried to kill myself once when I was 18 years old. But then I saw the damage that I did to my mom, and I said that I would never do that again, because it hurt her so much. There's nothing wrong with my mom—she's the best. I'm not going to take the coward's way out anyway.

"I was smart. I had 4.0 grade point average when I was in high school. I was very smart. I made it all the way through school and was never even suspended. I would call in, but I never ditched, so I didn't get in trouble for not being there. I liked school; I had cool teachers and I had a lot of friends and girlfriends. But I got high a lot, and I sold drugs. It's not all bad; my best job was doing telemarketing. I was confident and I had a good phone voice. I could push to sell like my mother.

"The last girlfriend I had got pregnant, and we were going to have a kid. We went out for one year, and she's the only one I ever loved. But she drank too much and had a miscarriage. We broke up because her family was racist and hated white people. Now I just sleep around, but I don't care. She's the only one I ever loved. A lot of people have left. When I was 12 years old, my grandpa died. When I was 13 years old, my uncle shot his head off. The next year, my other uncle killed himself. Last year, my niece was murdered.

"I don't want to end up a 40-year-old bum on the streets shuffling to the liquor store. If I get off on this arrest, I want to go to the community college and get my commercial driver's license. It would be the coolest if my dad were there and was teaching. I could take the class from him…but actually he could just teach me at home.

"Some of the best people I know I met on the street. The gangsters and drug fiends can be assholes. It's even worse if you're white and young.

Then you're the 'punk little white boy' and then I have to prove myself in every way. But I'm a dealer, and I'm a gangster. I have death warrants on me now. I know one is for $500, and it's because I stole from them. I stay in the park, abandoned houses, and with friends in decent areas. I still go down where they are, but they just don't see me because I'm Ghost.

"It's really rough on the streets. To survive on the street, you need both street sense and common sense. You can't just have one and not the other—you need both to survive. You have to always find ways to make money, and you have to always watch your back...always. I know my surroundings, at all times.

"I'm always hungry, I don't sleep comfortably outside, and once I was so cold that I couldn't walk for six hours because my feet were numb. You learn certain ways—to always have certain things like extra socks, blankets, clothes, and food. I've got canned food at the bottom of my bag here because you never know.

"Most of us carry weapons for protection. This is mine [David pulls out large switchblade and opens it up]. I have a gun, too, but not with me; it's hidden in a safe place. I've been stabbed twice and shot twice [shows his scars]. They're from a rival gang fight or from people I did wrong. All it did was make me cocky.

"I plan to straighten up. Through all of this, and through all of these years, I would 100 percent have chosen a different road. I can't dwell on the past; I just have to move forward and not stress out on the future. Don't panic. You have to take what you asked for. When it comes, don't stress it. You have to deal with what you did. I want to have a house and family. I don't want to beg for change. I usually have more than everyone else, and I have more connections, and they all get jealous, but I've begged. I'm very caring and loving. I care a lot about kids. If I got my life straightened out, I'd want to help kids."

Chapter 4

WHAT HAPPENS WHEN THEY LEAVE HOME?

Most young adults transition successfully from home to college or home to the workforce. That's largely because parents help prepare their children to live independently. But runaway youth are often ill-prepared for living alone. In many cases, it is because their parents did not groom them for productive independence. Mostly, these youth worked hard to survive the day-to-day crises in their homes, and did not have the luxury of planning and preparing for their future, or developing a healthy sense of who they are. These kids might end up at a youth shelter, go into state custody, reside in friends' homes, or move to the streets. And although they might not have prepared in advance for their new circumstances, most of them have enormous survival skills, and they manage to survive many situations while living on their own—situations that most people never have to face in a lifetime. For example, a 15-year-old homeless girl who is cold and hungry quickly learns to refuse an offer of shelter and food from a 32-year-old man who simply does not seem right. Though such an offer might tempt her, she knows to weigh the potential for serious physical danger against the discomfort of cold and hunger.

WHEN RUNAWAYS GO TO A SHELTER

The Administration on Children, Youth and Families estimates that 1.3 million runaway youth need shelter services, even though only an estimated 30 percent of the youth who leave home reach shelter programs

(U.S. House of Representatives, 1992). In other words, 70 percent of runaways and street kids never access a youth shelter. Even though shelters provide warmth, food, and security, most youth in need of such services refuse to voluntarily seek them. One reason for this reluctance is that shelters require children's parents or guardians to sign consent for services within 24 hours of their arrival. Although this requirement might seem benign, youth who have left home to escape abuse (physical, sexual, and/or neglect) or family conflict are often unwilling to have their parents alerted to their whereabouts. Contact of the parent by shelter staff will lead to inquiries regarding the suitability of the youth's returning home. The child has no reason to believe that his life will improve or that his parent's behavior towards him will improve when he returns home. After all, when he left home (or was told to leave), he perceived that all other options were exhausted. Most children do not leave home unless they feel that working things out with their parents is impossible.

In addition to not wanting his parents contacted, he might not know how to contact them. Some parents go to prison and lose touch with their children while there. Some parents die, and their homeless children do not learn of the death until years later. Some youth come from homeless families that are transient. That is, the child became separated from the family for a period of time, and the family moved on to the next city without him. If the child does not know where the family is, the shelter will turn his case over to the state Children, Youth and Families Department. And thus begins the process of becoming a ward of the state, which is as aversive to many street youth as returning home.

Alternatively, the runaway child may already be a ward of the state and may have run away from state custody (foster or group home). He does not go to the shelter because his state-appointed guardian will return him to his previous foster care setting. Street kids sometimes report that they do not want to return to foster or group homes because of negative experiences while residing there. Four siblings who were removed from their parent's home were dispersed throughout the city into different foster care settings. The level of abuse those kids reported experiencing while in foster care overshadowed that which they received while living with their biological parents. Each child ran from his or her respective foster care home. The youngest sister began dating a man 15 years her senior and moved in with him. He was a leader of one of the most violent local gangs. Her social worker leveraged control on the child by refusing to release her monthly stipend unless she left her boyfriend. Unfortunately, leaving a violent gang leader who is physically abusive is not an easy task, especially for a dependent minor with few other resources. Without proper counsel and planning, leaving him had the potential to lead to serious physical harm. Thus, the child stayed with him. In sum, many children who leave state custody might also refuse to seek help at local shelters for fear of returning to system care. Many asked for help in the past but did not receive it, and they do not see the utility of asking for help again.

Shelter Services

Youth who access shelters are those who have not given up on the system or their families. Yet, even for those ready and willing to accept help, help may not be available. Although there are over 300 runaway shelters across the United States that receive federal funding through Title III of the Juvenile Justice and Delinquency Prevention Act of 1974, congressional testimony from the National Network of Runaway and Youth Services (1991) indicates that shelters for runaway youth are overcrowded and that there are not enough beds to serve all youth in need.

Kufeldt, Durieux, Nimmo, and McDonald (1992) noted that for those youth who do acquire beds, shelters appear to meet their short-term needs by providing immediate shelter, food, and supervision. Yet, there exists a gap in knowledge of long-term outcomes, including the effectiveness of shelter intervention in preventing future runaway episodes and improving family interaction patterns. Shelter programs have not yet documented the long-term effectiveness of their programs on the families and youth they serve, as that requires money to pay staff to follow up with clients after the clients have left the program. Thus, though youth who access shelter services receive immediate care, the long-term impact of shelter intervention on the family is less known.

Virtually no data exist that specify the treatment services received by youth and their families in these shelters (Teare et al., 1994). Shelters that receive federal funding are supposed to alleviate the problems of runaway youth, reunite them with families, encourage stable living conditions, and help them decide upon future courses of action (Grigsby, 1992). For example, New Mexican youth shelters provide individual and family counseling, educational and job-finding assistance, medical and psychiatric care, case management, liaison with juvenile justice programs, and assistance with Medicaid.

Even though shelters may provide additional help beyond meeting a client's basic needs of food, shelter, clothing, and medical care, many youth and families are reluctant to request other shelter services. Fear of further system involvement and prior negative experiences no doubt play a part. Also, this population is perceived as "difficult to work with" (Kufeldt & Nimmo, 1987). When assistance is offered, youth and families might appear uninterested, or might actively resist attempts from helping professionals. Family members might refuse to attend sessions, or might attend but remain uninvolved in the change process. Missed appointments and lack of follow-through are not uncommon.

Even motivated youth and family members may find that the shelter cannot meet their unique needs. Many shelters are not equipped to deal with youth who have substance abuse and mental health problems. Substance use and mental health problems are not easily separated from family problems, and many theorists suggest that running away from home is part of a larger behavior problem syndrome (Jessor & Jessor, 1977). Thus, in order to fully address running away from home and family problems, one must also take into consideration (and address) cooccurring problems.

When the unique needs of runaway youth and their families are addressed and problems they consider to be of utmost importance are the initial focus, engagement and intervention with these youth may progress. At times, however, counselors and social workers ascribe adultlike behaviors onto adolescents. This is not hard to do, as runaway and homeless adolescents have had to cope with adult issues and may appear precocious in some ways. Yet, these youth are struggling with very difficult issues at earlier ages than most adults. Also, they struggle without the experience and emotional support that most other teenagers possess. Professional training may help shelter staff effectively address the unique issues that runaway youth and their families face. Training should focus on developmental issues that adolescents face, family life-cycle crises and family psychology, techniques to engage youth and families into treatment, and specific research-supported clinical interventions.

Shelter Life

Shelters are organized so that when a child arrives, she completes an intake evaluation with a shelter staff member. During this evaluation, she is interviewed for suicidal and homicidal thoughts to determine risk for harm to herself and others. Her mental health needs and family, school, and legal history are probed. Youth who are at imminent risk to themselves through suicide, or are considered a danger to others, are not admitted to most shelters. A suicidal child requires inpatient hospitalization so that she can be more closely monitored and so that intensive intervention may be provided to alleviate her crisis. A youth with a history of violence could put other youth and staff at the shelter at risk. One gang-affiliated youth was admitted to a local shelter against the recommendation of some of the shelter staff. The child was known to carry and sell guns and to have a history of assault. He stored his guns in his closet at the shelter (unbeknownst to staff) and within one day assaulted another youth residing at the shelter. The police were called, and several warrants against the child for violent crimes were discovered. He ran from the shelter while police helicopters circled the area searching for him. Many shelter programs have few resources and are not staffed to address these situations, and are they neither able nor willing to take on the risk inherent in a high-needs child.

Once a child has been screened and admitted to the shelter, she is oriented to her room, kitchen, and areas within the shelter that she may visit. At this time, she is also told the rules of the shelter. Rules and expectations are often straightforward: complete required chores, respect staff and peers, no sexual relations with other youth, no drug or alcohol use, no threats or gang talk, and return by curfew. Shelters are structured to provide limits to children's behavior and consequences for rule violations. Many children from chaotic or disorganized families have not experienced this structure. For some, the structure provides comfort and stability. For others, the structure and rules are very difficult to follow, as they have become accustomed to their own way of getting through the day— without curfew, rules, or restrictions. Staff work with kids who clearly have trouble with boundaries and rules, and help youth learn new ways of behaving and communicating. Youth who do not follow the rules and have repeated violations are discharged from the program or leave prior to discharge (run away).

A shelter might provide new, positive experiences for youth. In addition to providing a clean, safe environment with clear expectations and a predictable schedule, programs may include weekly outings to the theater or recreational activities such as swimming, bowling, picnicking, and trips to the zoo or aquarium. Children can be provided a peek into the running of a functional middle-class family, with both support and behavioral expectations. Meals are taken together as a group, and outings are done in a group. Each child must negotiate conflicts with other children in appropriate ways, without the use of violence or threats. The child learns that she may talk to staff about fears or concerns she has about school, parents, or friends. In the evening, after dinner and any other planned activities, children and staff may flop onto the couches in the television room and watch movies or TV until bedtime.

In this era of managed care, most youth stay at a shelter for a brief time, between 1 and 30 days. During this time, the child's case manager strives to find a permanent, stable residence for the client. Most children residing at shelters eventually return home (approximately 90%). Not all youth return to their parents' homes, as some may be placed with a relative such as an aunt, uncle, or older, stable sibling. Depending on the resources available to the shelter, the staff therapist will meet with the family and youth prior to reunification. In these meetings, the therapist will help the family resolve at least the issues that led to the placement of the youth into the shelter.

As an alternative to returning home, youth who are at least 16 years old and who are able to maintain jobs and continue in school may apply to independent living programs. Here, youth are required to pay minimal rent, and the rules are more relaxed than those at a shelter or group home. Youth in these programs have curfews, need to prepare their own food, and may be required to participate in group therapy once a week. The transitional living programs help prepare youth for the responsibilities of living on their own, and many youth transition to their own residences from those programs. Children who do not return home or move into a transitional living program are placed into group homes or foster care settings.

WHEN RUNAWAYS GO INTO STATE CUSTODY

When an instance of abuse is reported to the state's Child Protective Services (CPS), the report is reviewed, and a determination to investigate is made. If the review determines that the child is in danger and is receiving inadequate supervision or care, the child may be removed from the home. In the case of two-parent families where one parent is the offender, the offender may be offered the opportunity to move out of the home in order to maintain the child in the home with the nonoffending adult. Removal of a child from home is the last option, although it may be the only option given the nature of the abuse. That is, if the abuse was so severe that remanding the family to therapy would not provide immediate cessation of the abuse, the child will be removed. If the family is mandated to treatment and further abuse occurs, the child will be removed.

Once removed from the home, the child may be placed into a temporary youth shelter until determination of his final destination is made. After completion of a full investigation, the child may return home from the shelter, or the state might start proceedings to remove custody from the parents and transfer custody to the state or another adult.

If immediate intervention is available through reporting abuse, why don't youth report it instead of running away from home? Some youth do not report abuse to authorities, such as school personnel, for fear that they may face repercussions from already angry, rejecting parents. Thus, the consequences of reporting abuse may cause many youth to avoid seeking help. Likewise, parents who abuse their children or fail to protect them from maltreatment may avoid contact with the helping profession to avoid a social service report or investigation. Even so, there is no shortage of reported child abuse cases. Three million child abuse incidents were reported to Child Protective Services (CPS) in 1999 (U.S. Department of Health and Human Services, 1999).

Criticisms of CPS

While the agencies of CPS exist to protect children at risk, there is a great deal of concern about the ability of CPS to accomplish that broad-reaching task (Munro, 1999). Some have suggested that the state may even serve as a source of further abuse to the child and family (Garinger, Brant, & Brant, 1976). Garinger et al. (1976) argued that the bureaucratic system of the state overshadows the interests of the child, and the child's needs are often ignored. In the 25 years since these charges were leveled, CPS has reformed many of its policies, and yet some child welfare analysts feel that CPS still falls short in its efforts to protect children from abuse and neglect (Waldfogel, 2000). Even fairly recently, it was noted that homeless youth are more often harmed than helped by the child-serving systems, and often leave system care when they conclude that the streets meet their needs better than the service system (Athey, 1995).

One disservice to youth is CPS's inability to provide stable placement. Studies of homeless youth consistently find that after CPS has removed children from the home, large proportions are shuffled from one placement to another (Shaffer & Caton, 1984). Melton, Lyons, and Spaulding (1998) criticize the social service system as a "slow bureaucracy" promoting an institutional climate, which intermittently retains children in restrictive settings for extensive periods of time, and then bounces them from one placement to the next. Researchers found that the average number of placements for older adolescents was 7.59, and that a high percentage of youth (63%) drop out of system care prematurely, highlighting the lack of appropriate placement services for older teens (McMillen & Tucker, 1999).

Studies examining the impact of system placement are needed in order to direct system improvement. The few completed studies delineate an increased risk for continuing problems into adulthood, including further system contact, among those with a history of childhood out-of-home placement. One study found that adult homeless women with a history of childhood foster care or other placement were more likely to have children who had lived in foster care (Zlotnick, Robertson, & Wright, 1999). As Haerian (1998) comments, children in foster care are often deprived of a sense of belonging and predictability, which may contribute to later maladjustment and behavior problems.

Potential System Benefits

Although system involvement may result in potential negative outcomes for system youth, we found some positive consequences for system-involved youth. In cases of serious abuse, removal of a child from the home may save her life. On a less extreme note, her removal and placement in foster care may provide her with growth-enhancing experiences that she would not otherwise have. She may be able to focus on schoolwork, eat regularly, and live in a loving, drug-free environment. In addition, the system has the potential to link family members to needed services, such as counseling or vocational rehabilitation, that they would not otherwise receive.

Slesnick and Meade (2001) found that longevity in the system was related to a lower incidence of attempted suicide. Future research may attribute the lower incidence of attempted suicide to greater monitoring of youth by system workers. Also, Slesnick and Meade (2001) found that system youth reported more use of prescription medications for psychological problems than did nonsystem youth. This finding suggests that system youth have greater access to psychiatric care and are receiving potentially needed psychiatric medications (primarily antidepressant and anti-anxiety medications). However, as system youth have few adult advocates, it is especially incumbent upon their health care providers to carefully weigh the potential benefits against the detriments of prescription psychotropic medications. Some medications, such as tricyclic antidepressants, may have potentially serious cardiovascular side effects on adolescents. Jensen et al. (1999), in an exhaustive literature review, noted significant gaps in knowledge about commonly used psychotropic medications for children and adolescents.

Some professionals believe that becoming a ward of the state has the potential to enhance a young person's life and future opportunities. Others argue that the system falls short of providing for the needs of its dependents and may cause more harm than good. Truth may lie somewhere in between these two perspectives. The system has the potential to both serve and mistreat its dependents, and how this service is carried out and monitored will depend upon those who oversee CPS, and on those who advocate on behalf of children without a voice.

WHEN RUNAWAYS GO TO A FRIEND'S HOME

A child who runs away from home might find temporary sanctuary at a friend's home. The friend's parent may have a long history in the runaway child's life or may have just met the child recently. Although there is a dearth of research in this area, four common scenarios are described below. These are based on stories told by runaway youth.

Scenario 1

The runaway child and her friend beg the friend's father to allow her to stay with them for a little while. The father has never met the runaway's parents and knows very little about her home life. The father allows her to stay in the home, but with the stipulation that her parents be told where she is. This is the recommended procedure for dealing with runaway youth who show up on a friend's doorstep. However, if the child reports that abuse is going on in the home and fears repercussions, a call to CPS is in order. CPS will likely initiate an investigation and advise the friend's father about how to proceed with the runaway child.

Scenario 2

The runaway has spent a significant amount of time at her friend's home prior to the runaway episode, and the friend's parents are aware of the conflict and problems occurring in her home. The runaway's parents have no problem with her remaining in her friend's home. In this situation, her parents do not want her to return home, and the host parents do not mind her staying with them. She may stay in the home for months and become inducted into the family. She may even flourish in this environment. For the first time, she may have regular meals and positive interactions with adults, and may be removed from an alcohol and drug use environment. However, over time, she will likely feel that she is not really a part of the family. Many kids said that they do not like feeling separate from the family they stay with. They have to ask for things in the home that the biological children do not, such as an allowance, and may sleep on the couch with no real privacy. They also notice that they do not get treated the same way as the biological children, and may begin to feel sad, angry, or resentful.

Abandonment by one's biological parents at an early age may drive even the best of us to behave poorly. A child might think, "If no one cares about me, why should I care?" She may be caught shoplifting, stay out late, use drugs or alcohol, or skip school. Now the host parents are faced with new problems. Clearly, the honeymoon period has ended, and the host parents are called upon to take on a disciplinary (parentlike) role, rather than a hostlike role. Some hosts may refuse the effort that this requires and so end the child's stay with them. Others may step up to the plate and attempt to rectify the runaway's problems.

In response to host parents who attempt to parent her, a child might respond in one of several ways. She might modify her behavior and begin to behave appropriately. Her behavior change will also depend upon the behavior of her friend (the host family's child). If the friend is a partner in crime, then the parents will not want to maintain a perceived negative influence on their child and will seek to remove the runaway from their home. If the host family's child is not engaging in problem behaviors and the runaway guest continues to misbehave, the host parents are also likely to seek alternate placement for the youth. The first call is usually to the runaway's parents, and the outcome of the call may include the youth's returning home. Or she may run to a different friend's home, and the cycle will begin all over again.

Scenario 3

In this scenario, the child stays at a home where she feels very comfortable and welcome. Her friend's parent feels protective of the child and has been involved in her life for several years. The runaway's father does not want her to be at this home and is angry about the other parent's harboring his daughter. The runaway's father may call and threaten the host parent, who has initiated the process to remove guardianship from the biological parent. Police may be called by either parent for any of several reasons. In this situation, both children and both sets of parents are thrown into a toxic battle that is unpleasant for everyone. In many cases, a runaway child's parent who fights to have his child back with him has not completely given up on the relationship. Such parents are often open to intervention and working things out with their children. Though the children may protest and suffer lingering pain from past insults, most children prefer to be with their own parents.

Scenario 4

Some children leave home and rotate among friends' homes for months. Host parents may not even know that the child has run away from home (or has been asked to leave home). The runaway will remain in the home one to two nights, and then transfer to another friend's home. Our experience has been that such slumber party bouncers are more likely to transition to the streets from friends' homes than are the other youth.

Children who cycle to different friends' homes but stay for a long period are usually those who are reluctant to go to the streets. They are also more likely to seek system help. These youth generally have less severe substance use and other behavior problems than street youth, as they are able to maintain in households by generally following the rules and contributing to household tasks. Many also maintain their attendance in school. The youth who have more severe drug or alcohol problems, school problems, and behavioral problems do not last long in other families' homes, as the parents are unlikely to take on the responsibility of reparenting a high-needs adolescent.

WHEN RUNAWAYS GO TO THE STREETS

Some kids know others who live on the streets and will seek them out when they leave home. Others do not know a soul and are terrified at the prospect of living in doorways, on roofs, or in a stranger's hotel room.

All youth are at increased risk of serious harm while on the street. Harm comes in many forms. Street youth are preyed upon by older homeless adults and may be coerced to deal drugs, to prostitute themselves, and/or to become involved in pornography. Older nonhomeless adults also prey upon street youth. Some adults may be lonely and seek the comforts of young, impressionable, needy children. Some adults cruise areas where street youth hang out and seek victims for their pedophilic fetish. Youth may be lured by promises of safety, food, drugs, shelter, and unconditional love and care. These are seductive offerings to a needy teenager.

Living on the streets is harmful to one's health in other ways, too. The risk of HIV infection, hepatitis, and other sexually transmitted diseases increases dramatically on the streets, where prostitution and IV drug use are a part of life. Rape, in addition to being traumatic, is potentially deadly, as some rapists carry HIV. Youth engage in criminal activities while living on the streets, including robbery and drug dealing, which are also dangerous. If a street youth robs the wrong person, he might get killed. If he deals drugs to a desperate, penniless addict, he might get killed.

During his first days on the street, a kid might connect quickly with other street kids. There is safety in numbers, and there is potential for garnering more resources when more than one person works toward a goal. When sleeping in an abandoned building, two people can take turns sleeping and keeping watch. Without a partner, one person could sleep only intermittently because of the danger of being jumped.

A girl might connect with a boy who has a bad temper and beats her nightly. Or, she might hook up with another girl who seems nice and promises to look out for her, but then takes off with all of her money and clothes. Living on the streets is hard. One adult described his homeless experience as more traumatic than serving in Vietnam. He said the fights and violence, the trauma, the vigilance, the lack of consistency, the lack of sleep, and the loneliness were worse when he lived on the streets than when he was in the jungles of Vietnam.

Where Do They Live?

Homeless kids will sleep in abandoned buildings, on rooftops, in doorways, under bridges, in cars, in hotel rooms, or on the floor of a friend's apartment. In most cases, they will try to sleep out of sight of others so they will not be robbed or attacked. They will sleep out of view of the police so they are not harassed and told to move along. Some homeless youth report that they sleep during the day and stay awake at night for safety reasons.

What Do They Eat?

Homeless youth do not eat well. Many are malnourished and panhandle for money to buy food. Some trade sex for food or money, or engage in other illegal activities (e.g., shoplifting, drug dealing) in order to get enough to eat. These youth generally avoid the adult soup kitchens, just as they avoid other programs that serve adult homeless.

What Do They Do during the Day?

Some street youth sleep during most of the day, waking up in the late afternoon to hustle and use drugs. Some youth sleep at night and hang out at a drop-in center for homeless youth, where counseling, activities, food, and structure are provided, during the day. They may stroll up and down the streets panhandle or stop at coffee houses. A youth who is tired of street life might obtain a job and work at the position in order to save up money for an apartment. Others are simply unable to work because of serious mental illness and drug addiction.

Our program has observed great drama among street youth. Though many will band together against an outside threat, the alliances and coalitions within the group often lead to arguments and physical fights. Youth bond closely to one another, but if a disagreement or a perceived disloyalty occurs, mayhem will ensue. Each youth will band against the other, garnering as many reinforcements as can be mustered. These bursts are intense but often short-lived.

Loneliness on the Streets

Many researchers and those who serve street kids speak of a youth's street family, as youth refer to their brothers and sisters of the streets. Yet, behind closed doors, youth will speak of the loneliness and the lack of connection and trust with anyone on the street. Though a child will develop a partnership with other kids on the street, those relationships are functional, as each person provides a survival function to the other. The partnership may serve a protective function, so that each watches the other's back. For instance, if trouble with another person occurs, the friends can unite against the threat and win more easily than could one person alone. Groups of partnerships may form. For example, one case involved three street partners who were all drug addicted. Two youth remained in a hotel room, while the third turned tricks or hustled money for drugs so that he could return and all could get their drug fix. Each took a turn hustling while the other two rested. Our observation has been that partnerships form quickly and dissolve quickly. The stress of living on the streets is not amenable to forming long-lasting, stable friendships. Loyalties are questioned, disagreements arise, and arguments ensue.

A child may state that he enjoys living on the streets and would not wish to have any other lifestyle. In fact, recently, a local news station sent a reporter to the streets to experience the life of the homeless. In the report, homeless people were interviewed, with a few individuals stating emphatically that they love the streets and would not live any other way. Although this statement might be interpreted as pure bravado, one can also interpret it in other ways. First, if non-street living is impossible for the person because he cannot maintain an income to support himself, or complete the activities of daily living (personal hygiene, bill paying, shopping, driving), then most likely he has a substance use or mental health problem that interferes with his *ability* to live life in the mainstream. Second, if the alternative to living on the street is living in a home where he is physically beaten nightly and sexually molested by his mother's boyfriend, then living on the streets would be a reasonably better choice. For him, the streets are a lesser hell than the home.

Health Care on the Streets

Wright (1991) concluded that homeless people are more physically and mentally ill than their counterparts in the general population. He examined the health care problems of homeless teens as serviced by Healthcare for the Homeless with a sample of 1,691 teenagers between the ages of 13 and 19 in 17 U.S. cities. Among the acute disorders, upper respiratory infections, skin ailments, and lice infestations were most common. The more chronic disorders included vascular disease, tuberculosis, gastrointestinal disorders, poor dentition, and nutritional deficiency disorder. Homeless females were shown to have many problems related to pregnancy.

Wright concluded that health problems of homeless youth were further complicated by the lack of access to medical care, poor compliance with the treatment regimen, and generally unsanitary and unsafe living conditions. De Rosa et al. (1999) surveyed 555 street youth in a service-rich area of Los Angeles, California, and found that only 28 percent reported accessing medical care services. The youth reported that drop-in style centers were accessed the most easily and adult shelters the least easily.

Service Utilization

When working with the homeless, case management needs to be provided along with treatment services. With a group that is residentially unstable, flexibility and accessibility has to be maintained. Practically, this means that service providers and researchers must be willing to work with youth on the street, in clinics, or wherever the youth may be located. Marshall and Bhugra (1996) note that outpatient therapy appointments are a low priority for the homeless person who needs shelter and food. If his basic needs are not met, he is not going to expend energy to address issues related to his homelessness. Discrepancies between perceived needs by the homeless and by mental health professionals can create a dichotomy that leads to a rejection of the services (Herman, Struening, & Barrow, 1993).

Many cities have programs that employ outreach workers to engage youth into programs. Outreach workers may travel in a van to areas where street youth hang out. Many will hand out care packages, including juice, food, toiletries, and underwear and socks, and information on where youth can go to get help. Outreach workers become known by street youth, and trust develops over time. A child is not likely to accept a referral to a drop-in center or treatment program without knowing that the worker does not have ulterior motives.

In general, street youth do not seek help for their situation. Research has documented very low service utilization among runaway and homeless youth. One study showed that only 9 percent had ever accessed mental health services (De Rosa et al., 1999) and only 10 percent to 15 percent had ever received treatment for alcohol or drug problems (De Rosa et al., 1999; Robertson, 1989). Among shelter-residing youth, service utilization may be higher; Slesnick, Meade, and Tonigan (2001) found that 29 percent of their shelter-based sample had accessed psychological services, although rates of drug and alcohol service access were comparable to rates found by other researchers. These youth may avoid seeking services because they perceive them to be judgmental and inflexible, as suggested by Marshall and Bhugra (1996) to be the case among homeless adults.

Low service utilization may be explained, however, by a lack of available treatment. Numerous barriers to treatment must be overcome in order to provide services to this population. Practical considerations must be addressed before treatment can commence. The very nature of being a runaway youth involves isolation from caretakers who could facilitate the procurement of treatment. Lack of insurance or transportation and the high cost of mental health services can impede these youth from receiving treatment. Adolescents covered by their family's managed care or private insurance provider may not be able to access those resources if contact with their parents is severed. Or, if they are avoiding detection by their parents, these youth may spurn using their family's insurance because it will notify parents as to their location. While some adolescents are covered by Medicaid, many runaway and homeless youth residing at shelters come from families with earnings too high to qualify for Medicaid. And although runaways living on the streets do have access to Medicaid, they often do not access Medicaid coverage (English, 1999), presumably because they have no address to provide, or are unaware that coverage is available.

Alienation from society and family may preclude these youth from seeking and receiving treatment. Runaway or homeless adolescents can become disaffected from a world that has yet to offer help or hope, and hence they may be resistant to overtures of assistance. Considering the lack of empirically supported treatments offered to these youth, the mental health field has not adequately served this population, and may be deserving of their mistrust.

SELMA'S STORY: THE TRAVELER

Selma was passing through Albuquerque, New Mexico, trying to get back to Berkeley, California. She had only a short time to talk with me because she wanted $80 for a bus ticket, and needed to get to the bus station to panhandle before it got too late. She was a beautiful young woman, but life on the streets had taken its toll. She had four large tattoos on her forearms and upper arms. Her hair was disheveled, and it appeared to have pieces cut off randomly around her head. She had not bathed in several days. She was outgoing and friendly, though she was reticent. When she told her story, she paused frequently and only continued after reassuring prompts from me; it seemed that she did not want me to see her in a negative light. Her body language and hesitation suggested to me that she was insecure, and she said that she has been unhappy for a long time. This is her story, in her words.

"I was born in Bosnia/Herzegovina, the old Yugoslavia, on June 1, 1981. I have a half brother and sister. During the war, when I was 13 years old, I became separated from my parents while we were being bused to refugee camps. The United Nations paid for me to go to the United States because of the war. Although they tried to help families, I was scared and crying because I missed my parents. But I knew they were taking me to a safer place. If I had stayed, it would have been more dangerous for me.

"When I got here, I felt like everything was gone or taken away from me, like my friends, family, and my home in Bosnia. I was crushed. I cried a lot and I heard things in my dreams. Right before I would fall asleep, I heard voices whispering in my ear and I felt air on my ear. The voices would whisper my name. That just happened a few times though.

"My mom was a janitor and my dad . . . I'm not sure about his profession. They separated when I was three years old and I didn't know much about him. My stepdad was a salesman. But, I grew up with my grandparents. That's why it wasn't that weird to separate from my parents during the war. You see, when my parents divorced, my mom got remarried. My stepfather's mother didn't allow me in her house, which is where they were all living. She wouldn't let me live with them because I wasn't her son's child. So when I was five or six years old I lived with my grandparents, who didn't live too far from my mother. Usually, I saw my mom almost everyday, but sometimes I didn't see her for a week or two.

"My grandfather worked for an import-export company, and my grandmother was a nurse. After a while, my grandma stayed home because she retired. Basically, she was my mom. I had a good relationship with my grandparents. My grandpa adored me. He always gave me money. It was the same with my grandma. All she talked about was that I was the one thing in the world that she cared about. I believe that we had a telepathic connection because I had meningitis when I was three years old, and my grandma was crying at the same time that I was screaming for her in the hospital. We just had a really strong connection.

"From the age of 10 until age 13 I moved in with my mom and stepdad because they moved into their own place. I wanted to live with them really bad because I loved my mom, and I wanted to be around her. She had just had a baby, and I wanted to be with my little sister, too.

"My relationship with my mom was more like a friendship. It always seemed like we were competing. She had a really short childhood and was not ready to be a mom. She was 18 years old when she had me, and she would hit me with a belt buckle, and she drank a lot, too. She was either working, out with her friends, or out with her family, and I wasn't ever a part of it. Every time I did something that was bad, which was little kid stuff, like crying because she had to leave . . . she'd hit me. I think I did that stuff for attention, and I'd also break stuff. I'd break all the toys I had. I didn't have much respect for things, and I gave away or destroyed everything because I wanted attention. Those things didn't matter to me because I just wanted my mom. I envied my toys because she offered me material things only, and that's not what I wanted. So yeah, she hit me maybe twice a week, or gave me a whipping with the belt buckle, or threw me across the room, or pulled my hair. My stepdad abused me more than my mother.

"My stepdad would come into my bedroom at night and cut my hair off in chunks. He was an alcoholic. He was not really sexually abusive, but he would touch me wrong. Like, he would wake me up by putting his hands on my chest and shaking me. He also punched and kicked me, and knocked the wind out of me. He started to do that because I started to have bad grades, and I wanted to hang out with my friends. I always felt like I was walking on glass in front of him—anything would piss him off, and he'd freak out. There was a lot of psychological abuse. He'd call me names and made fun of my ears. I was insecure, and he'd go out of his way to make fun of me. He always told me that I'd never amount to anything.

"Before I left my family to come to America, when I was 12 years old, I ran away from home. I'm not sure anything specific led to that. I just remember wanting to go hang out with my friends, and so I didn't come home for a week. My best friend was Alexandra, and her parents were kind of wealthy. She and I would hang out a lot and get in trouble together. We would smoke cigarettes, drink alcohol at parties, and skip classes. Then her parents banned me from hanging out with her. So we both ran away together. We didn't go far. We went into the shed next door to her apartment. We locked ourselves inside, and it was a very tiny space. We had a Walkman, food, and a flashlight, and we stayed inside that shed for two days. We talked about how great it was not to have pressure from our parents anymore. She went home after two days, and I went to another friend's house and stayed there five days. They didn't call my parents until I wanted them to. I heard that my parents were worried though, so when my friend's family called my parents, they weren't mad. They were glad that I was alive, and they said that I better not ever do that again. So I didn't, but I came to the States without them.

"When I got to the States I was automatically emancipated. Another family and I went to Salt Lake City, Utah, because that state accepted us and allowed us to live there. I got my own apartment, a part-time job at a grocery store, and I went to high school.

"School went bad. I was disinterested, and I was all alone. It was different because all of my friends went home, and I didn't have a family to go home to. I had friends that were like my family though. But I started getting bad grades because hanging out with my friends was more important to me. I was really depressed. It was the worst time of my life. I missed my family, and I didn't know what I was doing here on planet Earth. It didn't seem like there was a point in anything that I did because I was never going to get what I wanted, which was love and a family. Now, I talk to my mom about once a month. It's strange because we have grown apart. I still love her though, and I hope to see her some day. My grandma passed away right before I came to the States, when I was still in the refugee camp, but I didn't find out until I got here. I was devastated. She was the only person that understood me and cared about me.

"I'm not sure I ever pulled out of the depression. I dropped out of high school in the beginning of the eleventh grade. I guess I got out of the depression eventually, but it cost me a lot. I don't have a high school diploma, and I feel like I wasted a whole bunch of years. I wasn't saving money then, and I don't think I was prepared to be on my own at the age of 14 (I turned 14 at the refugee camp because I was there for three months waiting for the papers so that I could come to the U.S.).

"In the eleventh grade I quit my job. I stayed in my apartment until the lease was up, but I had no money or anything. So I just decided to travel. I hitchhiked to New Hampshire. It was kind of scary having to talk to strangers and not knowing if they were crazy or not. There are a lot of weird, perverted people out there.

"I was in New Hampshire for four months. Friends of my family from Bosnia are there, and they had a daughter my age. I thought maybe she would be someone I could be friends with, but she didn't like me, and didn't want to hang out with me. Really, she was a snobby brat. I just realized that they weren't my friends after all and I left. They fed me and were nice, but after a while it seemed like I was starting to get on their nerves. They'd say to me, 'So what are you planning on doing?' I went back to Salt Lake City; I was 17 years old then.

"I moved into an apartment with one of my really good friends, Paul. It didn't work out because I didn't get a job. It was really hard to get one. Eventually, though, I got one. But I missed my opportunity to get a house with my friends, so I was kind of out there. I went to live at my friend Angel's house with her mom and sister and their little baby. I helped them out by cleaning and cooking so that I could stay. I stayed there for about two months and left because I met a boy. I moved into his house—he was 24, and I was still 17. He worked at a skate shop, and I stayed with him a couple of months, but we decided that neither one of us was ready for a relationship. We both needed to work on our lives instead of trying to be together. I was young, and didn't have a job, and we were both really scared.

"Then I moved in with my friend Robert and his parents. He had a big giant house with a pool table. The house was constantly messy because he had a bunch of brothers. It was a Mormon family, and the mom was against me being there because I was a girl and it wasn't appropriate for a female to live with a bunch of boys out of wedlock. But I lived there until I was almost 18 and left because I wanted to get a job and my own place. I wanted to establish something.

"Then I met my friend Katie. She lived with her family, and she was a crazy punk rocker girl. I had a crush on her when I first saw her. I consider myself to be bisexual. I didn't know that I was bi until about two years ago, when I was 19. I had a girlfriend once, not Katie though. It was the same relationship as if she was a boy, except that her body was different. Also, the reaction she got out of me was a lot different than if I were a boy. She made me get really defensive and jealous, and I was more negative about things. She cheated on me practically in front of me. Girl relationships are more psychologically negative, like me and my mom's relationship. Maybe there's something to that, but I'm not sure.

"Anyway, Katie's family adopted me. At that time, I was smoking more weed and drinking more alcohol, which I started when I was 14 or 15. I lived with them for one year. That was the longest that I lived anywhere. It was fun because we had the whole basement to ourselves, and we used to hang out at a coffee shop all day and wrote and played. She worked at a child care or day care place, but I had lost my job as a shoe salesman. I figured it was a lost cause, so I decided to get out of there. I was just depressed and destructive.

"I hopped a train from Salt Lake to Las Vegas, Nevada. I traveled with my friends Jesse and Jamie, and we slept on rooftops in Vegas—I was 19 years old. We were in Vegas for two or three days and then went to Santa Monica, California. I was there for about a month. That's where I did heroin for the first time. I got hooked and was injecting it. After about three months I quit cold turkey because I could not find anymore veins and I didn't want to muscle it. I was thinking, 'This is screwed up! I don't want to do this anyway.' Basically, I had an epiphany. I also panhandled for the first time when I was in Santa Monica so that I could get money to eat. I didn't need money to sleep because I was sleeping outside in the bushes, on the beach, anywhere.

"From Santa Monica I went to Portland, Oregon. I met a kid there, and me and him hitchhiked to Seattle, where we did more heroin. I still smoked weed, too. At that time I smoked weed regularly. I was in Seattle for one month and hitchhiked by myself to Salt Lake. That was the scariest experience of my entire life. I didn't know what I was getting into. I wanted to get home because I was sick of being dope sick. There were lots of emotional things to deal with, and I was not really thinking. I had the urge and energy telling me that I had to go. It was scary. The truckers that I got rides from had swords and knives nicely displayed. I had nightmares that they'd stab me. Fortunately, nothing happened. They'd ask me to show off my attributes, but I refused, and I was lucky that they gave me a ride anyway. I think I'm really, really, lucky.

"From Salt Lake I went to St. Louis, Missouri, then back to Salt Lake, and then to Minneapolis, Minnesota. I got engaged to this guy, and we were both working at a place in Minneapolis. I actually knew him from Salt Lake, and we moved to Minneapolis together. I was there for six months. I left him because he was starting to get abusive. He'd push me, shake the bed while I was sleeping, and yell and scream things at me. He was 27 and I was 20. So, I moved back to Salt Lake. Later, he came back to Salt Lake too, and we both moved to Portland. When we got there, I left him again because he didn't trust me. I stayed there for about eight months though.

"I got involved with a boy from work in Portland. We broke up because he was a rebound relationship for me, and I was needy. I went to Boston with another friend, and I was drinking and smoking every night. That friend took off when we got to Boston and stranded me with no money. I was stuck with no money, but I got a job at an art store. I met a lot of great people my age who let me stay at their house. We'd drink, smoke pot, and watch movies. After about two months I moved from there back to Portland. I had a friend in Portland who wanted to play music with me, so I saved up my money to go back. I play the drums, well, actually I play all kinds of music. Music is the most important thing to me. I played in a two-piece band for about five or six months, but the boy who I was playing with fell in love with me, and I didn't want a relationship after all the other bad relationships that I'd had. I told myself that I had enough and that I needed time to do things.

"He ended up punching me in the head because we didn't have a status—we weren't boyfriend-girlfriend. He wanted that really bad and I didn't. He was just frustrated because he was not getting what he wanted. I got a job at a tavern in Portland, and I was really stoked because it was the first time that I wanted to get my own apartment and get back into school. I worked really hard. But all of my friends would come over to my work, and I'd give them free beer. I got caught, and they fired me.

"The day before I got fired, I found out that I had the opportunity to get a room at a friend's house for $200. I didn't know what to do. I only got $180 on my last check because I had to pay back the beer I gave out, so I didn't have enough to move in. I looked around for a loan from friends, and I couldn't get another job (it's hard to get a job in Portland). So, some friends were leaving for San Francisco, California, and my friend Annabelle and I decided to go. We packed enough to survive on the street-clothes, a toothbrush, a Walkman (a must), sleeping bag, canned food and fruit, batteries, and a notebook (for my diary).

"We went to Berkeley and ended up staying there for a while. We went to Oakland and stayed at a warehouse which was rented by a bunch of skater kids. They had ramps set up like a skate park. That was really fun, and I was there for about a month. It was fun because I met intelligent and interesting people. The people there were really friendly and were interested in just hanging out with us. I didn't feel like they were just wanting to help us, they genuinely enjoyed our company. When I was there, I protested to shut down the docks because they were shipping war material to Iraq in Oakland. I got beat up by the cops really bad.

"I went all the way down to Santa Monica for the second time. It was kind of weird because I was doing drugs there before. I wanted to get out of there really fast, and bused from there to Pomona and got a ride from there to Tempe, Arizona. I was traveling with my friend Mike who is just a traveling partner. We rode with two hippie mommas to Albuquerque. Mike went off in Tempe to some other woman's house, and I met two kids in Tempe who came with me here to Albuquerque. I've been here for two weeks, and I have been panhandling on Central Avenue. I've been staying at a camp next to the railroad tracks that a Cuban guy showed us.

"I want to get back to Berkeley because my friend Mike is there...and it's the only place that I want to go. I can get a job there. It's better for homeless kids because it's easier to get help and money. They have a Magical Drop-in Foot Wash for all the homeless kids. They give massages and all kinds of food. You cannot go hungry or get hurt there. People prey less on the homeless and there's a lot of friendly people. Plus, I have people I can stay with (the kids at the warehouse) until I get on my feet. My long-term plans are to have a family, and someday I want to play music in a band. I want two kids, three at the most. My street name is Anomaly because I feel like one. I just feel like I'm a different breed."

Part II

TO THE PARENTS

Chapter 5

WHEN YOUR CHILD RUNS

The development of treatments that focus on adolescent problems has lagged behind those that focus on adults. For example, within the substance abuse treatment literature, in comparison to over 1,000 alcohol treatment outcome studies with adults (Miller et al., 1995), Williams and Chang (2000) were able to locate and review only 53 empirical studies investigating the relative effectiveness of substance abuse treatments for adolescents. Even less attention has been given to the treatment of runaway and homeless youth. Nevertheless, many professionals have been serving and treating runaway and homeless youth and their families for many years and have learned about the family patterns associated with running away. These professionals also know from experience what works and what does not work when intervening with these families.

Parents might have one of several different reactions to their child's running away. In cases where the child runs infrequently, the guardian might respond with terror, fearing for the child's safety and hoping for his or her expeditious return. These parents might call parents of their child's friends, or they might search throughout the city, combing popular hangouts and surrounding streets.

WHAT YOU MIGHT BE FEELING THE FIRST TIME

Children can provide the greatest joy in life and the greatest heartbreak and sorrow. The emotional impact of a child's leaving is intense. Many emotions wrapped up together make it hard to separate one feeling from another. One of the most common and dominant feelings that parents describe is feeling alone in their struggle with their child. Most people have never had the experience of a child's running away and do not understand the situation. You may detect a hint of judgment in others' attempts to console you. Adding to parents' feelings of isolation is the perceived lack of guidance and support from social service agencies. Many parents complain that, for the most part, mainstream mental health and community service providers do not seem to know how to advise parents, and parents do not know what options and services are available.

The first time your child runs away from home, you might panic, visualizing scenarios of pain, victimization, and terror for your child. You might envision your child holed up in a smelly room, involved in drugs with friends of ill repute. Perhaps you worry that your child will be taken advantage of by older adults who prey upon vulnerable, scared teenagers. You fear that your child will leave the state and you will never see him again. Worse, you fear he will be abducted. All of those fears are normal for parents who love their children. The fear is especially intense when coupled with helplessness. The feeling of not being able to rescue your child or simply not knowing what to do can frustrate even the most unflappable person.

In addition to fearing for your child's safety, you might feel that you have failed in some way, and question your own parenting. If a fight led to your child's leaving, you might be replaying the disagreement in your head. It is always easier to look back and see how things *should* have been done.

Although everyone makes mistakes, the handling of those mistakes differs dramatically among people. Healing happens through recognizing and acknowledging mistakes and moving forward to repair losses, rebuild trust, and tap into that well of underlying love and care that has become obscured by the many painful interactions over the recent months or years.

Shame may creep into the picture, too, and affect your actions. Calling parents of your son's friends to ask if he is there seems like a logical step. But asking the question admits vulnerability. The parent on the other end of the line might think the question is an invitation to provide advice or to tell a story of his own. Also, your question might provide more intimate family information to near strangers than you would like. Yet, calling other parents is the only way you will know for sure if your child is at their home. Fear of judgment versus fear for your child's safety has to be weighed. Many parents are overwrought with anxiety about their child's safety. Shame, fear of judgment, and embarrassment become secondary to panic and horror regarding the child's situation.

Some parents report feeling embarrassed: "A troubled child means that our family is dysfunctional and that we are not able to keep the family together." You might feel reluctant to ask for help outside your family and friends. Perhaps asking for help makes you feel that you cannot handle the problem yourself—and that means you are a failure. Although some families may feel that way, another interpretation is that you care so much about your child that you will try anything that might help. It takes courage and strength to face a problem head on and to seek help. It takes even more to admit that the problem involves everyone, and that everyone needs to be involved in the solution. The problem ceases to become his or hers, but becomes ours.

You might feel sadness for the loss of your child who slipped out the door, and wish for simpler times when he played with his blocks and followed you around the home begging you to play with him. The runaway episode represents more than the physical loss of your child (however temporary); it might also represent the loss of innocence and even hope. You might think, "How did it ever get to this point? Nothing I do works ....I give up." These feelings are normal. Remember that, though times are strained now, many families get through this crisis and repair old wounds. The relationship did not deteriorate overnight, and likely it will not heal overnight either. It takes time to rebuild trust to return to the old affectionate ways.

You may be angry, even furious, at your child for running away and again throwing you into a state of despair and anguish over him. Doesn't he understand what he puts you through? Doesn't he care about you? Doesn't he know how much you care about him? You might be surprised to learn that your child is probably asking the same questions. However, you might be even more surprised to learn that your child may not have any idea of the impact he has on you. The anger you two have shown each other has hidden the underlying hurt and desire for closeness.

When you find that your child has left, you might not know what to do or where to turn for advice and information. Frustration may set in when you call service programs or the police. In smaller cities especially, you might be told that nothing can be done and that the professional on the other end of the phone does not know how to advise you. However, that professional might refer you to another agency, which will refer you to another program, which will refer to you to yet another. You might also be told different things by different agencies. One agency representative says you should call the police, while another tells you that it will not do you any good to call the police. One professional offers to meet with you to prepare for the child's return, while another will not meet with you until your child returns home. What do you do? In the end, you must proceed with what you feel is right for you and your family.

WHAT YOU MIGHT BE FEELING DURING SUBSEQUENT RUNS

After one or more episodes of your child's leaving home, you are likely to respond more calmly than you did the first time. After all, you have been through it before. Some of the more primal fears—that he will surely be killed—are much more subdued because he has survived prior runaway episodes. This calmer reaction does not mean that you do not care; it simply means that the terror is gone. You begin to accept that you cannot always be present to protect your child and that he is going to make decisions that you cannot control.

A pattern might develop over several runaway episodes. You now know what to expect, and that expectation reduces your concern. The pattern may be something like this: You come home, and your child is gone. He later left a message for you, letting you know that he is okay. A week goes by, and you return home to find him waiting for you. He says that he ran out of money and needs to rest and shower. You let him in, and he cleans up and naps. You make dinner and eat in silence. He stays home that night, but leaves the next day, and the cycle begins again. It is a similar sequence of events every time.

Other scenarios abound. You may not hear from your child for months. Perhaps the pattern of his return is through the juvenile justice system, as he is arrested for shoplifting or drug-related charges. When he runs, you may have to pick him up a few weeks later at the juvenile detention center.

If your child follows a pattern, the runaway episode can be much less traumatic. However, feelings of hopelessness and sadness may grow with each runaway episode. It may seem that no matter what you try to do to prevent him from running away, he still runs. You have tried counseling, you have compromised, you have rearranged your schedule to spend more time with him and monitor him. No one likes to feel as though the situation is hopeless. Frustration mounts when help is limited and no one seems to understand what you are going through.

WHAT YOUR CHILD MIGHT BE FEELING THE FIRST TIME

The first time a child runs away from home, some of her feelings will be similar to yours. Family members sometimes lose the sense that other members feel pain, hurt, or tenderness and instead attribute malicious intent to each other. Although it was likely different in the past, after years or months of arguing and disappointment, concern and caring become secondary to criticism, disappointment, or indifference. Because it is easier to be angry than hurt, anger is often a primary emotion for both the parent and child.

At the core of many children's experience is the belief that their parents do not love them or, at the very least, do not like them. Children believe this because they can see their parents' anger but not their underlying concern and fear. Parents, on the other hand, know that even when a family member is angry with another, a foundation of love still exists. Thus, youth might feel particularly devastated and hurt after an intense argument. And intense arguments often precede running away from home.

The circumstances under which the runaway left will also provide some information about her feelings. If you and your daughter had an argument immediately before she left, her runaway episode was likely spurred by impulsivity and anger. She may not have adequately planned where she would go and what she would need to survive. Chances are she will return fairly soon—when the anger fades. If she left in order to spend more time with her boyfriend (something that you would not give permission for), then anger is probably not as prominent. More likely, she feels indignant because she perceives that you do not respect her and her independence. She might rationalize leaving home as her right to be a full-blown adult.

If crises in the home accumulate over time, or if physical or sexual abuse occurs, then leaving is the runaway's way of coping with the home situation. She has left home feeling sad and alone. She might even meet other kids on the street or adult outreach workers who encourage her to return home. They will tell her about the perils of living on the streets and that it is hard work. They will tell her that she will be cold at night and that she will be hungry. She might be told that she will be chased out of parks and restaurants by unsympathetic adults. Though well-intentioned, these advisers will not have success in convincing her to return home. Excitement about the possibilities and about being away from potential trauma at home most likely prevail. She has made up her mind to take her risks on the streets instead of taking certain abuse at home.

No matter what her reason for leaving home, during the first runaway episode, she might question whether she made the right choice and worry about how her absence affects you. In light of the crisis, she yearns for the time when you and she were happy together, when you and she did not always argue. She yearns for the time when you laughed together. Guilt might reinforce her feelings that she causes you trouble and hardship.

Many parents find that hard to believe, and vehemently deny that their child experiences any compassion towards them or has a desire for a better relationship. In fact, children who run away from home are thinking the same thing about you—that you do not want them around and would be happier if they were out of the house. Both of you find it hard to believe that the other misses the tenderness and fun that were once part of the relationship.

Youth who run away often report that they miss and worry about siblings they left behind. Runaway youth may feel as though they have abandoned their younger brother or sister. Sometimes, the runaway child will communicate with a sibling after leaving home. In cases where the siblings are close and the runaway child does not communicate with siblings, there is sure to be resentment from the younger siblings when the runaway child returns.

The runaway may fear the unknown and being on her own. After the initial excitement of being away from home fades, most children begin to experience the reality of being alone. No longer can they depend upon an adult to meet their needs. At this vulnerable point, they may be most likely to consider returning home, where they know the environment and where they can meet their basic needs for food, rest, and medical care.

WHAT YOUR CHILD MIGHT BE FEELING ON SUBSEQUENT RUNS

After previously surviving on her own, the fear of the unknown lessens. She may now know where she can find food, and might even have discovered a social network where she can receive support and emergency care. This network might include other youth who live on the streets, or agencies that serve the homeless. If she has run away more than once, each time away from home may become easier; and if so, it may be less likely that she will return home permanently. As the initial fear of being on her own and feelings of guilt or regret diminish, she becomes less and less likely to return home and work things out with you and the rest of her family.

WHAT YOU CAN DO

Although perhaps easier said than done, staying calm is a worthwhile goal. Though you may feel frantic and out of your wits in worry, your child probably has more survival skills than you may know. If she has made the choice to leave home, she likely has a plan, for the short-term at least.

Youth who go to the streets are at more risk for being victimized than those who go to a shelter (Kipke, Simon, Montgomery, Unger, & Iverson, 1997; Whitbeck, Hoyt, & Ackley, 1997a). However, most youth do not go straight to the streets the first time that they run away from home. Most first-time runaways go to a friend's home or to an older acquaintance who has an apartment. Some might get in a car and drive to another city with a friend, stay in a hotel, then turn around and return home.

In the midst of the crisis, try to take care of yourself. Sleepless nights and fretting to the point of making yourself ill will not serve you, your child, or your family. Do what you can do for your child, and then call upon your own support system. Engage in activities to help you stay calm. Perhaps watch television, read, knit, cook, or exercise to relieve restless energy. Talk about your feelings to someone you trust. Sharing the weight of the burden with others can relieve you of some of your pain.

And how do you find your child? Any of a number of strategies might work for you. Different parents try different things. What you decide to do will depend upon your goals, comfort level with each option, and parenting and life philosophy. But there are no guarantees, and no one strategy works for every family. Each family has different needs, expectations, and rules. One family might bring in outsiders (other families, police, therapists, etc.) to help with the crisis. Another family, not trusting outsiders, might prefer to handle everything on its own.

If you are inclined to bring in outsiders and call for community help, you can call the police. Then at least your child's absence will be on record, and the police can keep an eye out for him. In some states, running away from home is illegal, while in others, it is not illegal unless the youth crosses state lines. If the police find your child and you refuse to pick him up, you might be charged with abandonment. Until minors reach the age of 18, parents are legally required to care for them unless arrangements for their safety, care, and supervision have been made. Sometimes, parents who are very angry or frustrated can negotiate with the police for the child to be transported to a runaway shelter. At a shelter, he has appropriate care and supervision, and you and he can receive a respite from each other.

If your child is already on probation, you can contact his probation officer. Running away from home might be a violation of his probation expectations, and a warrant can be put out for his arrest. Often, parents report having mixed feelings about initiating a warrant for their child's arrest. On the one hand, if he is picked up on the warrant and is in the care of the justice system, he is off the streets and in a fairly safe environment. This is an especially attractive option if you know that your son or daughter is in a high-risk situation, such as staying with friends in a high crime and drug trafficking area. Once picked up on the warrant, your child will eventually return home and will likely have more monitoring imposed through the juvenile justice system. Though this option removes your child from immediate danger, he might feel intensely betrayed that you called the cops on him. He may say that he will never trust you again. You must make the decision to call the probation officer based upon your own conscience and your relationship with your child. If calling the police and initiating a warrant for his arrest will remove him from danger and will return him home for a new start, then it is likely the right choice. If you do not want him exposed to a detention home or involved in the justice system because of your experience or fears regarding the system, then initiating the warrant may not be the right choice for you.

You might also call the parents of your child's friends to see if she is staying with them. Friends may know where she is and can at least let you know that she is okay. Your call also serves to alert friends and parents of the situation. They can be vigilant for her.

Although most youth do not attend school during the runaway episode, some do. You can go to the school and check with the main office for your child. If she is in school, you can wait outside her classroom until class ends and greet her. Another possibility is to involve the school guidance counselor, who might take your child out of the classroom and meet with the two of you. A child who continues to attend school, even in the midst of leaving home, is a child who still maintains her responsibilities and has not lost sight of her future and goals. This is a good sign, and intervention is often easier in that situation.

Those youth who work might continue going to their jobs. Even if your child does not continue to attend school, she may recognize the necessity of maintaining an income. Again, this is a good sign. Checking her workplace is a good idea if your goal is to talk with her and encourage her to return home. You can ask the manager if she has been coming to work, and if so, you can ask him to have your daughter call home. You must weigh whether you need to tell the manager anything else. Simply asking if she has been to work will probably be enough for you to acquire the information that you need. Telling the manager the situation may taint his or her perception of her stability and thus her job performance. You may unwittingly harm her position at the workplace.

Teenagers with e-mail accounts might continue to check their e-mail, especially if they have a network of friends with whom they chat at home or e-mail regularly. Even homeless youth have e-mail accounts that they access at libraries, coffeehouses, and homeless service agencies. In fact, this is the new high-tech way that service providers keep in contact with street-living youth. One recommendation is for you to e-mail your child that you miss her, are worried about her, and would like her to contact you to let you know that she is okay. Similarly, if she has a cell phone, call and leave a message.

If you have already called the police and friends and checked work and school, and you have not found your child, you may be feeling particularly hopeless. Parents often report that they cannot sit at home and wait for their child to return home. These parents feel they must do something—anything! You might be inclined to climb into your car and search for your child. If this strategy is one you feel that you must take, then you might find the following recommendations helpful. First, take someone with you. If you are searching through dangerous neighborhoods—neighborhoods that your child is known to frequent—do not put your own safety at risk. This precaution is especially important if you are searching at night.

Second, take a cell phone with you in case you run into trouble somewhere. Many cellular phones have an automatic speed dial feature that can be programmed to dial 911 by simply holding down the programmed button.

Third, have a picture of your child with you, and show it to people who are in the area where you think your child might be. Make it clear that you are a parent who is worried about your child, and not an undercover policeman, bounty hunter, or collections agent. Most people will be able to differentiate a frantic parent from a calm, cool, and collected hunter. Nonetheless, the street often protects its own. If people from the outside come to the streets, the homeless will protect each other's privacy.

Fourth, leave those with whom you come into contact a phone number where you can be reached in case they come into contact with your child. Fifth, check hotels, parks, and restaurants where teenagers are known to congregate. You can sometimes find out where they congregate by asking a youth you see.

When your child runs away, making a call to a family therapist may also be helpful. In contacting a counselor, you can alert the therapist to the crisis and receive potentially helpful advice or support. Some therapists may want to meet with you right away and begin the preparation for your child's return. The therapist should provide support and set up an emergency meeting. You should be advised that if and when your child comes home, a transitional therapy meeting will be arranged. It might be best not to address the running away incident with your child until this therapy meeting. This delay might prevent further conflict and facilitate a smooth return home.

Engagement should include identifying fears about meeting with the therapist. The therapist's first task is to establish a trust relationship with both you and your child, which will include a description of the therapy process and negotiation of goals. Clients' concerns may range from reactions to past negative therapy experiences to steadfast anger and refusal to be vulnerable again to pain. The therapist needs to explore your concerns about meeting with your child, and your child's concerns about meeting with you. Youth often report that they feel that there is no reason to meet with their parents because nothing will change. They may also report that they feel that the adults (the parent and therapist) will gang up on them, and they will be outnumbered. The therapist has to address this.

Some parents may have concerns that their own substance use or history of abuse may arise. The therapist needs to be proactive in addressing this, as this fear can lead to a refusal to participate in treatment. In most cases, therapists do not clamor to blame or find fault with any one person. Rather, the therapist should frame the meetings as a collaborative process in which everyone works together, regardless of the past, to repair relationships and begin to build a positive future.

Chapter 6

CONTINUING CONFLICT

In a perfect world, your child would never run away from home; the entire family would work through disagreements calmly and peacefully. A group hug after each family negotiation would be eagerly anticipated. In a perfect world, you would only agonize over which university will best meet the needs of your progeny. In the real world, however, running away from home is not particularly uncommon. Children run away from home every day, and parents long for their safe return. Perhaps you have tried the strategies laid out in chapter 5, and you found your daughter. Perhaps you told her you miss her, you are worried, and you would like her to come home now. What do you do if she runs in the other direction as soon as she sees you? What if she says, "No!" in response to your pleas for her to return?

WHAT YOU MIGHT BE FEELING

When you want something badly and cannot have it, frustration often sets in. Anger might mask the frustration. You might think, "I go through all of this effort to bring him back home, and he won't even come with me! Let him be out there alone!" Under some circumstances, giving up, at least for the moment, may be your only choice, and a good one at that. Giving up at the right time ultimately might help you meet your goal—your son's return home. Imagine your son screaming at you while saying, "Get the !@#* away from me! I hate you and never want to see you again!"

Although trying to tap his underlying love for you in the face of his anger might tempt you, giving up and returning home alone might well be the best choice. Pushing him to respond to you calmly when he is livid could exacerbate the problem. He is not ready (or able) to talk with you rationally or to hear what you might have to say. You might need to give him more time to let his situation (living away from you) and your request (to return home) sink in. It may take some time for his anger to dissipate.

A common reaction to a child's refusal to return home is hurt. You might feel abandoned and rejected. You put yourself on the line when you asked him to return home, and he rejected your overture. He tapped those insecurities you have about being loved and valued. He may not be aware he did that, but nevertheless you still feel abandoned. Children are not always aware of the impact they have on their parents' feelings. Even teenagers do not always believe that their parents can feel rejection, hurt, and self-doubt. Many only believe that their parents have powerful feelings of anger and condemnation. Likely, children believe this because of parents' higher status in the family and social hierarchy. Also, some parents may not share more vulnerable feelings with their children.

If your child refuses to come home, you might fear that you will lose him forever, that he may never come back, and that your family will not be whole or have a chance to heal. The potential loss might remind you of other losses in your life, or the loss of your own family of origin when you were a teenager. Although children are supposed to mature and move out of the home to begin their lives, a cloud of resentment, anger, and negativity should not characterize the move. Nor should the child leave unprepared for independence, or before you have prepared yourself for your child's absence from the home.

Self-doubt might creep into your head with questions such as, "What have I done wrong? What could I have done differently?" You might begin to question the things you said and did to your child and worry that you made the wrong choice in one situation or another. Take heart. Many parents question their abilities to parent their children, and you are no different from millions of other parents. And like those other parents, you must realize and believe that you did the best you could under the circumstances. Maybe you learned from mistakes, and you are hopeful for the future. Do not let memories of the past prevent the realization of your hopes for the future. In other words, acknowledge to yourself that perhaps things could have worked out differently, but that you are not going to give up on the future.

Though frustration and hurt might be prominent, patience and hope are the keys. In the face of this crisis, patience and hope might elude you. Remember that you can influence the situation, but you cannot control it. Work to stay calm when you think you cannot take another night with your son gone. Continue living your life as normally as you can, getting through your day, eating your meals, and taking care of your other children. Others depend upon you to take care of them, and without patience and hope, how could you keep your anger, frustration, hurt, and pain contained? Without moderation of negative emotions, your ability to carry out other life activities and responsibilities are compromised.

WHAT YOUR CHILD MIGHT BE FEELING

Your daughter's refusal to talk with you about returning home, or her flat-out refusal to return home, is probably motivated by several emotional factors. These emotions might include anger, excitement, shame, pride, guilt, and fear. She might not be aware of her own feelings. She knows that she is angry or upset, but labeling and understanding her feelings is more difficult. (It is difficult even for resourceful adults.)

If you successfully contact your daughter soon after she runs away, her driving force might be anger. Anger keeps her going strong, rooted in her belief that she is doing the right thing and can survive anything on her own. She might not be able to reason with you or hear what you have to say to her, even if what you have to say is that you miss her and love her. She has not had sufficient time to make sense of everything. She runs on adrenaline, enjoying the excitement of change and her newly found freedom and power.

In addition to the exhilaration of being without parental control, her refusal to come home at your request is downright intoxicating to her. Now she, and not you, holds the power. She has something you want—her presence! And only she can give you what you request (unless you send the police to pick her up). It feels good to have control and to have power over your feelings. What she doesn't realize is that she has always held the power to influence your feelings. For her, this is new. For you, it is old.

Shame? You might wonder what she has to feel ashamed about. Shame might motivate her refusal to come home because of the things she did to survive on her own. If she has been raped or beaten, she might blame herself for it. Perhaps she shoplifted or contracted a venereal disease and does not want you to find out. She does not want you to love her less than she thinks you already do. The best way to prevent you from finding out what she has done or what has happened to her is to avoid you.

In her mind, coming home at your request is an admission that she is guilty or is fully at fault for the problems between you, and pride prevents her from returning. If she knew that she would not be blamed, that she is loved and accepted no matter what, it would be easier for her to return. Unfortunately, she probably does not know how you feel, and you will probably need to tell her. To her, returning home might mean that she has failed, yet again; she could not even take care of herself on the streets.

Guilt might prevent some youth (and even some adults) from facing their demons. If someone does not have the support system or emotional resources to honestly examine his or her perceived bad behaviors, then guilt will win over. Your daughter may know very well that she has hurt you and that she jeopardized the safety of her younger sister by dealing drugs out of the home. The level of remorse is so unbearable to her that she cannot tolerate even the thought of dealing with her issues head on. Dealing with her issues means that she has to talk to you about them, which for her is a risk and potentially too painful.

If she experienced physical or sexual abuse in the home, it is possible that she will never experience self-doubt in regard to her decision to be on her own. She will continue with the conviction that she is doing the right thing, even after anger dissipates, and will take her chances on her own. Her resolve to stay on her own might be motivated by fear of further abuse. Her resolve might be reinforced by the perceived betrayal or lack of protection from you or others. Pure survival instinct might strongly motivate her to stay away from home.

With the exception of severely abused youth, most children who run away from home want to have better relationships with their parents (Teare et al., 1992). Runaway youth report that better communication with their parents is very important to them (Teare et al., 1994). Moreover, lack of contact with their families and, hence, the loss of the family relationship is related to adjustment problems, including depression and suicide attempts, among runaway youth. Most likely, your child cares about you and wants to come home. Sometimes, this is hard for her to admit to you because in so doing she becomes vulnerable, she is at your mercy.

As a child, she is without the same resources that adults possess. She does not have the power to sign her own lease without a guardian's cosignature, and has fewer means of survival than an adult (employment opportunities, public assistance, etc.). She likely does not have the self-assurance and the problem-solving and coping skills that an adult possesses by virtue of having longer to develop such resources. No doubt, she will question her decision not to return home. How long this takes will depend upon her personality and the home situation. Certainly, she wants to know that you do not blame her for everything that has gone wrong in the family. She wants hope; she wants to know that you care about her and love her no matter what she does. In the end, she is still a child. Although she behaves in adult ways, she does not think like an adult, and she does not have the insight that you have.

WHAT YOU CAN DO

If your child refuses to return home because someone in the home abused her, removal of that person from the home is an option. With the abuser removed, the home is safe again, and your child will probably return. If the alleged abuser is another child in the home, then counseling for that child and the family is advisable. If you do not believe that your child was abused by anyone in the home, then counseling is still advisable, because allegations of abuse are an extreme and dangerous way to garner attention.

Throwing up your hands and vowing to the world that you have had enough might feel good in the short term. However, the family interaction and therapy literature tells us that the only way to face a family crisis successfully is for family members to resolve the issues that keep them from being happy together. This means meeting together to talk about the painful things that are hard to hear. Running away from home is an interactional problem. In other words, it is not simply a problem that your child has, or a problem that you have. It is a problem of negative interactions between two or more people. Thus, in order to resolve the situation, the interaction between family members needs to be addressed. If the issues are ignored, your child's return home will be a springboard for him to leave again.

If he makes the choice to return after days or weeks of your unwavering and patient requests for him to return, then your family is in a good position to make some changes. That is, the situation is aided by the desire to stay together. Each family member agrees to work through the problems that initiated the runaway episode. If your child does not want to participate in working through these problems, the situation is much harder to address simply because the desire and motivation to change is not present in one of the key members. Alone, you cannot fix the situation; you need your child to meet you halfway. Perhaps, you also need the support of your life partner.

What if your marital or life partner feels differently about the situation than you do? If he feels less inclined to have your child return home, then conflict between the two of you is possible. Perhaps he believes that your daughter will learn a better lesson by staying on the street and suffering the natural consequences for her behavior than she would at home. If your partner is not your child's biological parent, you might question his motivation for not wanting your child home. This might occur if much of the conflict before your daughter left home revolved around him. The two never got along; she does not accept him, and he does not seem to like her. Or, he may have a very different parenting style than you have, and reconciliation of the two styles has proven difficult. What if your child yells defiantly, "I am not coming home until he is gone!" Are you supposed to choose between your child and your lover? Now, not only are you faced with the stress of your child being out of the home, but you are also experiencing relational stress with your partner.

Conflict might occur if your partner wants *more* done to facilitate your child's return. Perhaps your partner is the biological mother. You want to let things play out with your son, and she wants you to call the police, search the streets, call friends, and so on. This is not the first disagreement you two have had about your child. In fact, arguing about your son has become the main topic and mode of communication between the two of you in recent months or years. You might believe that if your son were no longer in the picture, you and she might be able to have a relationship without constant bickering. You might start having fun together again. Worrying about your son and discussing the problems that involve him would no longer dominate all conversations.

If your runaway child refuses to return home because she does not like your life partner, but your partner is not abusive, then sitting down together and hashing out the differences is necessary. The opportunity to resolve misunderstandings and expectations that each person has for the other sets the stage for starting again on a positive note. Sometimes, expectations are not clear. A child knows her expectations, and you know yours, but you do not know each others. For instance, you might assume that your daughter accepts your life partner as a parent and will follow instructions from him or her as she does from you. However, your daughter has a very different expectation. She does not accept your partner as a parent figure, and so does not respond to his or her parenting attempts. This has to be discussed if her return home is to be successful (i.e., that she will stay home). You will need to decide whether you require the support of an objective third party (a counselor) to help your family resolve this issue.

If your daughter refuses to return home even after all of your pleas, short of tying her down, throwing her in your car, and boarding up the windows in your home, there is not much you can do at the moment. However, you have made contact with her, and that contact communicates that you care and that you want to try again. Even if she does not return now, if you avoid threats and instead speak with kindness and acceptance, she will likely initiate contact with you.

What can you say to your child when she resists returning home? You can say, "I'm glad I found you; I have been very worried about you. I'd like you to come home now because I want us to work things out." You can also say, "I miss you, I don't want anything bad to happen to you out here. Nothing is so bad that we can't work it out. You know I love you, right? Let's go home now." Do not ask her to come home with you because the question gives her an invitation to say no. If she responds angrily to you, then you might want to respond with, "I know you're angry right now. We have a lot to talk about, but if you don't come home with me, we won't be able to work it out."

If she is still angry and is clearly not going to return home with you, then you can say, "I can't force you to return home with me because if you want to leave again you will. However, I want you to be safe. Will you stay at Aunt Tanya's house until we can work it out?" Aunt Tanya's house can be substituted for another family's home. If you do not have family in the vicinity, you can propose taking her to a shelter where at least she will receive the supervision and care she needs. If all of these efforts fail, then you can let her know that you will wait for her to call you if she changes her mind. Let her know that you want her to call you, and that you will come get her as soon as she calls.

Here is the tricky part. If running away from home is a crime in your state, you worry about her safety, and she refuses to return home with you, then you can call the police and give them her location. The police will pick her up and hold her at the juvenile detention center. She will then have no choice but to return home with you, and that directive will have come from the police, not from you, which can be used in your favor. After all, she is coming home because the police made her, not because you forced her. They are the bad guys, not you. She saves face, since she did not ask to return, and you save face because you did not directly force her.

WHEN YOU DO NOT WANT YOUR CHILD
BACK HOME

Some parents have reached the point where they do not want their child living in their home any longer. As noted earlier, when authorities become involved, these parents might be officially charged with abandonment. If parental guardianship is removed and no other relatives wish to take guardianship, the child will be placed in state custody and may be placed in foster care. But without abuse or neglect charges, this rarely happens. Other options for the child include transitioning into an independent living program or placement in a group home.

You might feel hopeless, frustrated, and angry with your runaway son. You might feel as though you did everything you could for him, and you no longer want anything to do with him. Your reluctance to have him back home might include (1) fear for your safety or another family member's safety, (2) fear that he will negatively influence other children in the home, (3) fear that you cannot handle him any longer, or (4) belief that he would be better off without you. Let's look at these concerns.

If your son has a history of violence, does not successfully control his rage, ignores your calls to the police, and refuses to participate in counseling, your reluctance to have him home is understandable. You want a safe home, and it is your responsibility to provide a safe environment for your other children. Perhaps everything you do seems to make him more angry. Everyone in your home lives in fear, not knowing what will set him off. When he becomes enraged, he seems like a different person—not your little boy, but a wild animal! Perhaps his absence from home is pleasant. You and others in the home do not miss him, though you feel guilty for admitting that. The home environment has been peaceful, relaxed, and normal. Though you still love and care about him, you and other members of the household would much rather live in peace than in fear.

You might have mixed feelings about his return if you believe that other children in the home will be exposed to his bad habits. Bad habits might include smoking cigarettes, using drugs or alcohol, violating curfew, cussing at you, and defiantly refusing to do his chores and go to school. If he is the oldest child, the younger children cannot help but marvel at his rebelliousness. Your youngest son might tell you that your older runaway son is cool, and he might try out some of his brother's bad behaviors. For the first time, your youngest son tells you that he does not want to go to school, "Why should I have to go when Patrick doesn't have to go?!" You might have come home to find your younger son with the smell of smoke on his breath. No doubt, your first thought is, "If his older brother did not smoke cigarettes, this would not have happened."

You might fear that you can no longer influence your runaway child. He does not respect you or the things you say. When you lay down the law in an attempt to structure his time and limit his behavior, he acts out even more. For example, in response to an earlier curfew, he does not return home late; in fact, he does not return home at all! You feel as though you have exhausted all of your resources in trying to address the situation. Whatever you do, wherever you go, whatever you say does not help your son. You are in the throes of learned helplessness. That is, you have learned that you are helpless over the situation and that nothing you do matters. Those with learned helplessness stop trying to affect a situation with which they have had no success over a long period. Many people develop learned helplessness when they experience depression, but it can also develop when trying to make changes in your family.

You might believe that your daughter will thrive if contact with you is severed. You might feel as though you are not able to parent her in the way she needs. You have more faith in the system or your relatives than you have in yourself. Perhaps you are experiencing an acute major depressive episode. Getting out of bed is an immense effort for you, let alone chasing a runaway child all over town. Parenting, including monitoring your child, setting limits, and maintaining consistency and follow-through with consequences for limit violations, demands immense effort. Expending this effort is difficult for someone who is very depressed. Perhaps your substance use prevents you from helping your daughter with her substance abuse. Researchers know that reducing or abstaining from alcohol and/or drugs is more difficult if a family member also abuses substances (Dishion, Patterson, & Reid, 1988). You might feel that you harm your child more than you help her. You might see yourself in your child and remember that you were doing the same things at the same age. You remember sneaking out of the home and doing things that your parents did not want you to do. Yet you did them anyway, and your parents ended up washing their hands of you.

You might have difficulty admitting that you do not want your child to return home. Meeting alone with a therapist can provide a safe context for you to express those difficult thoughts. And you will likely receive validation for your frustrations and relief from keeping your forbidden thoughts a secret. The goal for therapy with you and your child does not have to include transitioning her back home. Goals might include repairing the relationship and planning the new, future relationship with her living some place other than your home. Paradoxically, in 90 percent of cases when a parent and child initially refuse to meet together because neither wish to reunite in the same home, but they agree to meet with modified goals, the parent and child end up living back in the same home.

Chapter 7

WHEN YOUR CHILD RETURNS HOME

When your child returns home, you might experience peace, tranquility, and harmony. For the first time in a long period, your family experiences cohesiveness; being together is fun and pleasurable. It is like old friends reuniting after not seeing each other in years. But these honeymoon periods are sometimes followed by the same troubles and conflicts that occurred prior to the runaway episode. When you and your child are reunited, you do not want to think about problems that could ruin the reunion. And yet, if the reunion is positive, it can provide the perfect opportunity to begin repairing the relationship while everyone's motivation is high.

On the other hand, some families experience the reunion as a return to the same old negative, unpleasant interactions. Perhaps you see no changes in your child since he left home. Maybe things are even a little worse. He got a taste of being autonomous and liked it. Leaving home reinforced his determination to do his own thing regardless of what you might want.

WHAT YOU MIGHT BE FEELING

If your daughter returned home with a renewed spirit, obviously happy to see you and the rest of the family, then you might experience some of the joy that you felt prior to the start of all the problems. Though happiness prevails, even immense relief (that she is safely home), in the back of your mind, you might still worry that problems will crop up again. You worry that addressing the problems will rekindle her fury of days past and that she will leave again in a cloud of anger.

Although the problems in recent months and years have distressed you and the rest of the family, the return of your child reminds you of the possibilities for the relationship. You see that she *can* behave lovingly and she *can* follow the rules you have set for the home. She no longer seems possessed by those strange adolescent hormones that force her to behave like someone you do not know. Rather, she is again sweet, loving, gentle, and kind, and considers your feelings. She helps with the chores, and even does things for you without being asked. She attends school and completes her homework each night. She considers your feelings and seems to know that you want all that is best for her, and she no longer perceives you to be the dictatorial enemy who was put on Earth just to make her miserable.

The first day or night spent together at home might be pleasant. Freedom from fighting and peaceful togetherness intoxicate the family. Perhaps conversations revolve around safe topics, those that cannot possibly lead to any sort of conflict or disagreement. For example, your daughter asks, "Did the dog finish her training with you?" You respond with "Oh yes, we went to the training school, and she even sat when I said sit! And the teacher was so surprised she came running over to pet the dog!" Conversations like these have healing power. Though they may seem unimportant and trivial, they help set a positive tone and assist in repairing damage caused by many past negative or hostile conversations. Perhaps it is the first pleasant conversation you have had with your daughter in a long time. The words are not so important in this kind of conversation. The tone and the emotional impact of communication that is not negative says much more, and lays the groundwork for trust and more intimate conversations.

No doubt, optimism abounds, given that your child is back home. You might feel hopeful that things will change for the better now that you and she are given another chance. Your optimism is fed by the ease of your interactions and by your daughter's apparent turnaround in attitude, respect, and behavior. Hope and optimism are great motivators for change. Without the belief that things can improve, making the effort to change would seem futile. If you believe and hope that things can improve, then working toward that goal is more tangible and meaningful.

For some families, the reunion might not be easily characterized as a happy one. Family members still have lingering resentments and lack of trust that no one wants to address for fear of destroying the peace. Compounding the strain between you and your runaway child is the fact that your other children might feel that all of your attention and emotional energy are directed toward the runaway. They might feel jealous of that attention even as they are unable to recognize that the lack of attention makes them unhappy. Instead, they resent their newly returned sibling.

Your child's return might trigger a bit of annoyance in you. For example, what if she is not better behaved? What if she still cannot bear to be in the same room as you and appears unchanged from the runaway experience? She takes her dinner and goes to her room without a word. She barely replies in monosyllables to your questions. You hoped for a happy reunion, but she seems to care less about being home. You might ask yourself, "Does this mean that things will never change at home? Does she *want* to live here? Does she hate me, or is she just a good actress?" The good news is that she is home, and even if she does not appear to appreciate all that you went through in her absence, you are in a much better position to make changes in the relationship than you were when she was not living at home.

The excitement, joy, apprehension, and hope may all work together to leave you confused. Sometimes having many emotions mixed up together makes it difficult to separate one feeling from the other. Having different emotions about her return may overwhelm you, and figuring out how to proceed might feel precarious. If you fail to do something that you should do, then things might blow up, right? If you do it, things might blow up anyway. You might think, "Should I talk about the problems? Should I set limits? Should I sweep it all under the rug?"

WHAT YOUR CHILD MIGHT BE FEELING

Just as you wonder how things will proceed with your runaway son's return, he also wonders if you are angry with him or happy that he returned, whether you are going to lecture him, praise him for returning, limit his behaviors even more, or ignore him. He does not know what to expect, just as you do not. Depending on his experience outside the home and his experience before he left home, he may happily return or, alternatively, do so unhappily.

If his experience on his own was bad (he missed his family and having his own room and his own things at his disposal), he is probably happy to be home. He wants to please you and hopes that you will forgive him. Like you, he hopes that things can begin again on a more positive note. The difference between how he feels and how you feel is that he may be less able to identify his feelings. The mix of emotions that you feel is most likely doubled for your son. He has less experience sorting out his feelings, and he may be less able to label his feelings. His feelings can change from one minute to the next. He might feel relieved that you are not angry with him, and so he does the dishes after dinner as a symbol of gratitude. But if you ask him a seemingly benign question, such as, "Did you tell your coach where you have been?" he might feel attacked and lash out with, "Stop harassing me! Why do you always jump down my throat with everything?" Not only is he trying to negotiate his relationship with you, but he struggles with his own feelings of self-doubt and failure.

Since he has less power in the home, given his status as a child—and a problem child at that—he may take his prompts from you. If he is excited and happy to return, but you appear angry and upset, he might subdue his outward expression of relief. However, if you are also excited, happy, and hopeful and show that you are willing to work together to address the problems, then he will be more likely follow suit. So, he might return home and not say very much at all. He waits to see how you will respond to him. Once he figures out how you feel, he will feel safe to express his own emotions, whether they include anger or relief. Some youth find it difficult to express their emotions because of the risk it involves. If they emote one way and you respond the opposite way, they may feel ashamed and will not risk showing that emotion again.

Even if your child returns home and appears unchanged and angry at all that transpired, this feeling is not set in stone. It might even be a cover-up for more vulnerable feelings such as shame and guilt.

WHAT YOU CAN DO

Knowing what to do when your son returns is not simple because different families must use different strategies. There is no list of right answers. Several different strategies might work equally well. How you decide to proceed will depend upon your relationship with your child, and no one knows that relationship better than you. If you try to do one thing and it does not work, then you can move on to the next option. Knowing your options, though, will help you decide what might work for you and your runaway child. Thus, in this section, several options are provided from which you may chose.

Recommendation 1

When your son first returns home, avoid discussions about potentially flammable topics. These topics include reasons he left home, where he was while he was gone, what he was doing while he was gone, and what you expect from him now. These topics should not be avoided forever, just in the short term. The reason to avoid these topics soon after his return is to avoid another argument that might precipitate his leaving again. The problem that initiated the runaway episode was not addressed during his absence, and it did not get resolved prior to his leaving (or he would not have left), so what is different now? Perhaps nothing. Or, attitudes and approaches to problem solving might differ from those that were prevalent prior to the runaway episode, making resolution possible. But right now, so soon after his return, you probably do not know if anything is different.

Recommendation 2

Interact if you can. The absence of arguing does not default to positive or even neutral interactions. Family members who do not argue may simply avoid one another completely. If interacting triggers heated arguments, avoidance is an appropriate solution for the short term. Perhaps avoidance as a general coping strategy developed over time is the only means to get through the day. Or avoidance may occur because family members simply have no interest in each other. All that was good in the relationship is lost, and the effort and desire to retrieve it are also gone.

The first step toward a better relationship is to feel comfortable being in the same room together. If your son avoids you, then you need to initiate contact. Because you have more authority in the relationship, you will have an easier time taking this risk than your son would. For example, if he is watching television, sit down and watch with him. You do not have to talk to him, just sit with him. If he is eating a snack at the kitchen table, get the paper and sit with him. You still do not have to talk. The message is clear. You are letting him know that you want to be in his presence and that it is safe to be together. Nothing bad will happen by sitting together. You have set the tone: safety, care, love, and the desire to be together.

Just because you make the effort to be with him does not mean he will respond in the way you want. He might get up when you sit down and go to another room. If this happens, do not address it, just let it go. He is too hurt to allow this level of closeness. Give him more time, and try the same thing later in the day or the next day.

Recommendation 3

If things are going well with your child, and there is no avoidance, take every opportunity to say positive things. The absence of conflict does not mean that positive communication occurs. In fact, research on couples shows that happy couples are differentiated from unhappy couples by the presence of positivity, not simply the absence of negativity (Gottman & Levenson, 2002). You will know that things are going well when he is open to being with you and to making changes. Perhaps he shows you this by going out of his way to help around the house, by being kind to his siblings and to your life partner, and by doing what he thinks will make you happy.

Strike while the iron is hot. He tells you through his behaviors that he wants the relationship to improve. Tell him over dinner that you missed him. Tell him that you love him. Tell him that you want to work things out so that he does not leave again. Saying these things to him puts his fears to rest and helps motivate him to continue his changes. Someone has to initiate kindness, and it is probably easier for you to take the risk of rejection than for your son. You have more resources and experience than he does to help you recover from the wound. Plus, you are more likely to know that he hurts than he is to know that you hurt.

Recommendation 4

Keep grounded. Your son might ignore your friendly overtures. As a response, you might avoid discussing problems with him (because he is still angry and avoidant). You cannot walk on eggshells forever. At some point, changes need to be made and communication needs to begin. In order for changes to occur, you need to prepare yourself for conflict and unpleasantness. Eradicate the underlying infection so the family can heal. The process might be difficult, but the outcome—peace and calm for the family—will more than justify it.

Alternatively, interactions between you and your son might be great. He might seem much happier and more easygoing. Still, do not expect that problems will never arise again. The honeymoon is unlikely to remain happy and carefree once the crisis (the return home) has passed. Problems that occurred before he ran away were probably a long time in the making, and they will require more than a few days to address and solve.

Recommendation 5

Once things settle down, a routine develops, and interactions between you and your child are fairly normal again, then it is time to talk about what happened prior to the runaway episode. As noted earlier, until the issues that led to problems are discussed and resolved, they remain burdensome to the relationship. They will fester under the peaceful surface like a building tornado. If, prior to the runaway episode, your son did not like your boyfriend, and the arguing and bickering between them increased to a breaking point, those issues are not going to magically disappear because your son ran away from home and returned.

You might wonder how you should bring up the problems that led to the runaway episode. Begin the conversation with an upbeat tone. You may say something like, "When you left, I was really afraid that something might happen to you, and so I don't want you to leave again like that. Let's talk a little about what happened, okay?" To minimize the number of disruptions, set aside some time when the television is turned off and the younger children are in bed or out of the house. Start with an open-ended question that does not create defensiveness, such as "What upset you the most before you left?" He would have a hard time interpreting that question as an attack. Yet, no matter what his answer is, remember to stay calm. Because you are the adult, it is up to you to set the emotional tone for the meeting. If you get upset, he will get upset. But if you stay calm when he lashes out at you, then you set the tone for effective communication, a tone that is safe, calm, and collaborative. By not reciprocating the attack, you might also be breaking a cycle. In the past, when he attacked, you attacked back. Then he struck back with greater force and venom.

This should be an informational meeting, a time when you can understand each other's feelings. If you understand his feelings, and he understands your feelings, then responding to each other will be easier. No longer will you or he attribute malicious intent to every question, comment, or behavior. If you know what is really going on emotionally with the other person, then you know that maliciousness is not a motivating factor, and each person will respond more benignly to the other.

For example, let's say that the event that led to the runaway episode was that he failed his math test again. He came home and did not tell you what happened. Instead, his teacher called to tell you he failed and might need to take a summer class. Because you know he can do better on math, his lack of effort makes you crazy, and you hit the roof. You ended up yelling at each other, and that night he slipped out of the house. But he didn't run away because you yelled at him. It is never a single event that sends a youth out of the home, and certainly not simply argument. More likely, he ran away because he thinks you believe he is stupid and a loser. Perhaps he'd felt that way for months. He interprets your frustration and anger as disappointment in him.

If he is 14 years old, he is probably less able than a 17-year-old to identify the reason he left. He ran away from home in order to test that you care about him, even though he fails his math classes. If your son is 16 or 17, he might be more aware of his feelings of failure. His feelings of failure might be compounded by his fears about what he will do when he turns 18 and moves out of the house.

Recommendation 6

Evaluate the need for outside assistance. If you are unsure how to proceed with your son, having tried several different strategies to pull him back into the family, then perhaps the time has come to contact someone outside the immediate family who can objectively assess the situation and facilitate a resolution. If your family is opposed to a mental health or school counselor, other possibilities exist. The outside person might be the pastor, priest, or rabbi from your church or synagogue. Some family practice physicians take special interest in the families they serve and might facilitate a family meeting. A neighbor, close family friend, or a family member living outside the home, with whom all members connect, could be helpful. Everyone needs to perceive the facilitator of the family discussion as neutral to each family member's position. If the facilitator favors the parents over the child, the meeting will be useless because the child will disengage (zone out) from everyone during the meeting. If the facilitator favors your child over you, you will discount her comments and certainly not invite her back.

The need to bring in someone from outside the home is not an admission of failure or a reason to feel ashamed. Rather it represents your willingness to do whatever it takes to help your family. The emotions you have surrounding your family can cloud your ability to rationally address the issues that your runaway child brings up. He may ask for changes from you, such as an extended curfew or more latitude in driving your car. Some of his requests might be reasonable. An objective third party can help you separate the reasonable from ridiculous, if all of his requests seem ridiculous to you.

Also, a third party might be better able to help your child recognize that some of his requests are unreasonable. Hearing from you that a midnight curfew is unreasonable does not carry the same impact as hearing from an objective third party. He knows that this third party is not trying to treat him like he is a five-year-old (as he might perceive you doing).

YOUR CHRONIC RUNAWAY RETURNS AGAIN

Your son's return might be the fourth reunion this year alone. The pattern of his return is as predictable as the pattern of his departure. No matter what you do, it seems to have no impact on the family situation or on his behavior. You no longer know what to do, so perhaps you do nothing. His return or absence does not signal any sort of change. You do not panic when he leaves or have much change of emotion when he returns. It is business as usual with him living at home or living elsewhere.

WHAT YOU MIGHT BE FEELING

You used to feel excited when he returned home. You felt as though you were given another chance, and that the two of you would work out the differences. Now, after so many reunions and letdowns, you feel no joy and no sadness when you think about the situation. In fact, you feel nothing. Numbness has taken over your senses. Your son is like a tenant, a stranger, coming and going from your home. The only difference is that you do not receive compensation for the room, and tenants might be kinder to you.

Perhaps you wonder if the reason for all the family strife stems from you or him. You might alternately blame yourself and him. Maybe you yelled too much, or maybe you did not spend enough quality time with him. Maybe he was born with a bad attitude, or maybe his friends corrupted him, and it had nothing to do with your parenting. However, as noted earlier, the cause of an interpersonal problem does not rest solely with one person or the other—otherwise, it would not be an interpersonal problem. In any case, searching for answers is a normal process for anyone who tries to understand and address stressful situations.

WHAT YOUR CHILD MIGHT BE FEELING

He feels just as numb as you feel. He keeps returning home even though he probably could survive on his own without you. Why does he keep returning? Although he does not know how to fix the relationship with you, he still wants a relationship with you. Unless he experienced severe abuse while at home, he will always want to know that you love him and care about him.

He might feel tired and depressed. Leaving home is hard work. Depending upon where he goes, he might not have enough to eat or access to a shower, and he probably feels like an outsider. He might feel love-starved, even though he does not show it to you. He certainly did not return home to torment you and make you as miserable as possible. If he starts a fight with you, it might be his only means of getting your attention. If you become furious with him, then he knows you still care. If you ignore him and walk away, he wonders whether you care, so he might increase the level of insult in order to hook you in to him.

WHAT YOU CAN DO

As the problems between you and your child are long-lasting and the cycle continues without hesitation, something new needs to happen. If you already tried (on your own) to address the issues that interfere with your relationship, then recruiting someone from outside the family to facilitate changes in the home might be worthwhile. Things could not get any worse, and there is the chance they will get better.

In the worst-case scenario, your child's return means that life will be miserable until he leaves again. You have not closed your home to him, but you consider that option now. If you tried everything that you can in order to develop a healthier relationship between you and your son, but still everyone is miserable, other options exist. Your family's home is not the only place that he can develop into a well-adjusted adult. If your home is chaotic, for example, and your son needs more attention, he may thrive at the home of a relative who has no children and a more structured environment. He will not fall apart, and neither will you. In fact, the change may positively affect everyone. The important part of a successful separation is for him to know that you love him and that you care. You can have contact over the phone or have weekly (or more frequent) visits. This can happen, although it will take time, and it may take hard work.

Chapter 8

KEEPING YOUR CHILD FROM RUNNING AWAY AGAIN

Now that your child is back home, you want her to stay home. You hope never again to experience the stress and agony you felt when she left. Preventive measures race through your mind. A tracking device? Impractical. A private investigator? Expensive. Lock and key? Inappropriate. If you've run out of ideas, don't lose hope. Practical suggestions, information, and procedures that might help you meet your goals are provided below. These suggestions on how to keep your child from running away again are more practical and acceptable than the use of tracking devices, private investigators, and incarceration.

EXPECTATIONS

Every parent and child has expectations of the other. In some cases, the parent does not know what the child expects, and the child does not know what the parent expects. Ignorance of another's expectations sets the stage for disagreements and disappointments. Why? Because if you do not do something that someone expects you to do, that person is likely to feel frustrated and upset. You might not understand why your daughter is upset simply because you didn't know what she wanted you to do. You might think, "If I didn't know she wanted me to pick up tickets for the hockey game, she should not be angry at me, and I do not deserve to be yelled at!"

Parents commonly expect their children to go to school and maintain good behavior and grades, return home by curfew, complete chores around the house, and remain alcohol and drug free. Your daughter might expect you to allow her more freedom or to be more lenient with school performance, curfew, or tasks at home. She might expect you to respect her right to choose her own friends, clothes, hair style, or piercings. She might expect that you will pick her up from school on time, allow her use of the car for important Saturday night events, and stay home with her on Friday nights if she does not have a date.

When the expectations you have conflict with those of your daughter (you want her home by curfew, and she wants more freedom), then you need to negotiate and compromise on the expectations. But everyone must agree to, and understand, the negotiated expectations. Do not view this as a win-lose situation. Instead, it is a win-win situation because everyone gets something.

Recommendation 1

Set reasonable expectations for one another. If your daughter was failing every class at school, you cannot reasonably expect her to receive straight As her first semester back in school. This is not to say that she is not bright enough or cannot achieve straight As. She might simply need to catch up with the material that she missed and develop a study routine, which might take some time: small steps toward a bigger goal. She is more likely to succeed with the expectation of a 2.5 semester grade point average and 90 percent attendance than a 4.0 average and full attendance. She will be more willing to accept an expectation that she feels is attainable. No one likes to fail, but fearing failure is almost as aversive.

If expectations are too extreme in other areas, such as an 8 P.M. curfew on a Saturday night for a 17-year-old, she will have difficulty agreeing to and abiding by the expectation. She will break the curfew (ignore the expectation), and the family will end up with a runaway child again. Her suggestions might also seem unreasonable. A 2 A.M. curfew for a 15-year-old is too late in many parents' opinion, and therefore is an unacceptable expectation.

Recommendation 2

Be sure that you and your child discuss your highest-priority expectations. You might not manage to cover every expectation, but cover those that lead to resentment and anger. An important expectation for your child might not seem important to you. So, when you ask your child, "What do you expect from me?" and she responds, "That you allow me to drink soda with dinner, and let my boyfriend Soren come to dinner," do not automatically discount her request. It might be important to your daughter even though it seems trivial to you. Allowing her to drink soda may signify to her that you see her as a young adult and not as a child. Inviting her boyfriend to dinner might signify to her that you accept him as part of her life and respect him. Through your respect for him, you show your respect for her.

IDENTIFICATION OF NEEDS

Needs and expectations might overlap. Your son might need attention from you when he returns home from school after a bad day, or even after a particularly good day. He might need to know that you trust him, that you think highly of him, and that you love him. He might need time away from the family on weekends. You might need time alone on the weekends, or you might need your son to eat dinner with you at night so that you feel you are still a part of his life. You might need to know that he is safe at night when he goes out with his friends. You might need to know that you still matter to him even though he is growing up and becoming more independent.

Identify needs by asking, "What do you need from me?" or "What do you want me to do more (or less)?" He probably will not ask you this question spontaneously, so tell him what you need: "I need to feel that I'm still a part of your life." Identifying needs is not usually enough to resolve the problem. You must discuss and negotiate how each need will be met, as described below.

COMMUNICATION

You and your son might have developed some negative communication patterns over a long period of time. These patterns must change if you want him to stay home. Right now, your conversations might be more notable for this anger than for expressions of care and concern. Perhaps the discussions focus on what is wrong with him and not on things that are going well with him. You never seem to laugh about funny things that happened during the day. No one teases anyone, and no one jokes. Opening the door to communication and chipping away at the walls between you will help keep him in the home.

Change requires practice, patience, and probably quite a bit of time and effort. If a conflict occurs that you cannot discuss calmly, the best tactic is to shelve the problem until you are more calm. Time away from the issue might create some perspective on it, and then you can discuss it much more easily. In your time away from the problem, decide if it is really as bad as you initially thought it was. Do you think your daughter dented your car because she has no respect for you and your things? Did she dent your car because she tries to make your life miserable? Probably not. She probably dented the car because she was not paying enough attention to the road—simple as that. Though you might interpret her behavior as a personal attack, in most cases, that is not her intent. If you can interpret the situation in a neutral manner, you will probably approach the discussion with a neutral tone.

What if you remain calm during the discussion, and your daughter has what appears to be an emotional breakdown and begins yelling and screaming at you? What if she storms off to her room, shouting a string of obscenities on the way? Easier said than done in some situations, but (1) do not shout back, (2) do not blame or personally attack her, and (3) do not follow her. What you can do is (1) stay calm, (2) say that you will discuss it with her later, and (3) take care of yourself—watch television, read a book, take a walk, or call a friend.

You might not understand why your daughter becomes angry with you when you have no ill intent toward her. It might seem to you that she becomes angry with you even when you are particularly warm and loving. When family members interpret comments as hostile that an objective observer would think benign, in most cases this is because they experienced several months or years of fighting, hostility, frustration, pain, and hurt. The cycle of negative communication can be broken. One tactic to assist in developing more positive communication is to reconnect with your empathy toward your child and practice perspective-taking.

Empathy and perspective-taking might be lost, but they can be found. The techniques described below might seem elementary, even silly. However, these are basic communication skills that are often taught to couples and families, and with proven effectiveness (Olson, 1993).

First, one person must talk at a time. Do not interrupt, and do not use body language that discounts what your son says. Even if you do not agree with him, listen attentively and calmly. When he completes his thought, repeat back to him what you heard him say. When you do this, he knows you heard him. Keep your mirroring of what he said short, and do not add your own opinion to it. This is harder than it seems. Many people, when asked to do this in a therapy session, mirror ideas, thoughts, and emotions that were not conveyed by the sender. Simply state what you heard him say, and ask him if you understood him correctly. If you do not do this, you run the risk of responding to something that was not said, but rather your interpretation of what he said.

Once you correctly mirror what he said, you can practice perspective-taking or empathy. You might ask, "And that is frustrating to you?" If he responds yes, you have made progress. First, you have acknowledged that you heard what he said, and then you connected with him by validating his feeling about the topic.

Next, ask your son how he would like to resolve the problem or issue. "What would you like to see done about this?" Then repeat back to him what you heard him say, and ask him if you accurately understood what he said before you move on. Once you understand the problem, his feelings about the problem, and his proposed solution, then you can respond. If you accept his proposal, then this communication exercise is nearly complete, and you succeeded. Thus, you might respond to him, "Okay, I hear that you do not like the 9 P.M. curfew, that it makes you feel like a child, and that you would like to have the curfew extended until 11 P.M. I am okay with that curfew, but I would like you to let me know where you are because I worry about you."

You can use this style of communication to discuss nearly any topic. Most people are not born with these skills, and the more you practice, the easier it becomes. Communication is difficult, especially when emotions are raw. Communication characterized by negative, angry, blaming, hostile, and defensive comments probably developed over a period of months or years. The cycle can be broken through changing attitudes about the other person and through concrete communicative behaviors. In fact, you can disagree with your son and feel strongly about an issue, yet still communicate effectively and productively about it. What happens if your son proposes a solution that you simply cannot accept? No need to despair. Negotiation and mediation have prevented many wars between nations, and negotiation can help resolve this situation, too.

THE NEGOTIATION PROCESS

When you and your son cannot agree and it seems that all the jewels and fruit in the world cannot bring you together, it is time to pull out those negotiation skills that therapists and politicians use so easily. Negotiation skills are needed when you cannot get what you want and he cannot get what he wants. Below are a few steps to follow so that both of you can get what you want.

Step 1

Include someone who is not emotionally attached to the topic of discussion. This person should lead the discussion and should not show favoritism for either you or your son. If favoritism is shown, the discussion will fail. The unfavored person will feel ganged up on and will leave the discussion. The person chosen to lead the discussion should not have any preference for one particular solution.

Step 2

Brainstorm with each other a list of possible solutions to the problem that you are discussing. No brainstorming idea is too ridiculous to include on the list. Brainstorming means that anything and everything should be written down. Both you and your son need to contribute to the list. If only one person provides the brainstorm solutions, the other person will not have ownership in the problem resolution process and might feel less motivated to succeed.

Step 3

You and he must eliminate absurd or completely unacceptable brainstormed solutions that clearly will not work: for example, "I get to fly to Grandma's house when we have a big fight," but Grandma lives in France.

Step 4

Gradually pare down the list until one solution remains. This solution might require some adjustments, and each person can propose modifications until an agreement is reached. For example, "Okay, I will eat dinner every night with you if you clear the table afterwards."

Step 5

Implement the proposed solution for a specified period of time—one week or one day, depending upon the problem.

Step 6

Everyone should meet again to revisit the problem and solution. Ensure that the proposed solution is working to everyone's satisfaction, or determine that another brainstorming session is necessary.

This strategy is versatile. You can resolve conflicts that range from curfews to homework. The procedure requires everyone to participate because everyone is integral to the solution. Instead of decisions handed
down from you to your child, solutions are created and developed so that
all feel their needs are met and their feelings have been validated.

ALTERNATIVES TO RUNNING

Sometimes one disagreement with you is all it takes for your son to
storm out the front door and not return home. Running away from home
might be the strategy your son uses to cope with anger. You must address
this with him. Everyone can remain in the home and learn to address conflict and disagreement in a collaborative, problem-solving manner. Your
son can remain angry with you and still live at home, though he may not
realize that. If he leaves, how can you resolve the problems?

You and your son must develop alternatives to relapse (running away).
This should be worked out together, because an alternative to running
away will succeed only if everyone involved in the alternative agrees to its
implementation. Identifying the best alternatives for your family requires
some digging. First, you must uncover the primary reason for the running.
Is he running away to get back at you? Does he run because that is the only
way he knows how to handle his anger? When he runs, do you end up
spending more time with him when he returns, so that running away is the
strategy he uses to obtain more time with you? Or is it the opposite? Does
he run to acquire independence because you involve yourself in every
aspect of his life? The list of reasons and reinforcements for running away
from home is long. Finding the alternative that fits both your and your
son's needs might require some creativity and planning. Developing a plan
now will prevent a lot of pain and heartache later.

Of course, the goal is for you to communicate so effectively that you
will not need to make these arrangements. Ideally, when you and your son
have a disagreement, you will both sit down, discuss it calmly, generate
solutions, and come to a resolution. Alternatives to running away from
home are for those times when the communication process breaks down
and an emergency plan is required. It is best to develop a plan before it is
necessary!

Option 1

If your son usually leaves home after an argument, arrange a safe haven
for him in the home as an alternative. This is a room where he can get

away from everyone. You and other people in the home must promise not to follow him into the room, and you should not request permission to go into the room when he is there. He can signal to other family members that he needs time alone by putting a sign on the door, although you might need to set a time limit for him to be alone in the room (e.g., three hours). The room allows him the opportunity to calm down and relax while remaining in the home.

Option 2

Arrange for him to go to a friend's home or another family member's home for the evening. Ideally, he should return home by bedtime. The message that you want to send is that you can have disagreements and still be together. No matter how much you disagree with each other, it is most important that you are together. A short period away from home can help you or your son calm down, but after five or six hours, the absence from home turns into avoidance.

Option 3

Instead of your son leaving home or isolating himself, you can leave home, with the understanding that he will stay home. You must determine how long you will be away, and let your son know where you will be and when you will return. This plan allows your son to remain home while you leave to take a break.

Option 4

If an argument triggers your son's leaving, then when the discussion begins to escalate to the point where people are no longer calm or able to problem-solve, someone can blow a whistle, signaling that the conversation must end and family members must disperse for one hour. At the end of the hour, everyone convenes in the same place to renew the discussion, but more calmly.

Option 5

With the help of your son, create a list of individuals he can call during a crisis. These are people who will listen to him in a nonjudgmental and supportive manner. A trusted counselor or therapist is a good addition to the call list. If your son calls the counselor, stating emphatically that he wishes to run away, then the therapist can negotiate to (1) have everyone meet together to discuss the problem, (2) meet alone with the youth, (3) meet alone with you, or (4) arrange for the youth to stay overnight at a runaway shelter, where he will receive appropriate supervision and care.

CONCLUSION

This chapter provided a range of techniques and strategies that might prove useful in preventing your child from running away from home. Identifying expectations and needs, combined with positive communication and a sound negotiation process, can interrupt negative communication patterns. When communication breaks down and family members need to separate from each other, developing alternatives to running away from home can break the cycle.

Chapter 9

WHEN SOMETHING GOES WRONG

Your daughter returned home, and you worked hard to make changes. You talked to her about needs and expectations, and you communicated with her using a nonjudgmental tone. Curfew, homework, chores, and independence or dependence needs are resolved. When disagreements occur, you address them in a collaborative problem-solving manner. You listen to her, she listens to you, and you reach an agreement. The tone in the household is similar to the tone when things were good. High levels of emotion are handled by taking a time-out from the conversation and revisiting it when everyone is calm. You sleep well at night, and your daughter sleeps in her room rather than on a park bench or on someone else's couch.

Just when you think that the family situation is under control, it happens. She comes home drunk or stoned, or you meet her new best friend who is not a friend you would choose for her. Perhaps you have an argument that is so intense that violence occurs. She hits you, or you hit her. Though these situations are very distressing, they are not novel. They happen in other families, too. Here are some suggestions for handling the situation when something goes wrong.

CHILD USES ALCOHOL OR DRUGS

The clock strikes 10 P.M., and your son stumbles through the front door. He slurs an inaudible response to your question, "Where have you been?" Or, you might notice a change in your son over a period of a week; his

eyes often seem glazed, and his movements seem slow. He is not motivated to do the fun things that he normally wants to do. Instead, he sits in
front of the TV in an apparent daze. These situations, which include personality change, obvious intoxication, or unusual behaviors indicate that
he might be using illicit substances or alcohol. Although you suspect that
he used drugs or alcohol when he ran away, you assumed that those problems went away when the family reunited. Unfortunately, the reality is
more complicated.

Experimentation with drugs and alcohol is statistically normal (Jessor
& Jessor, 1977; Rose, 1998), and many teenagers grow out of alcohol and
drug use. However, some teenagers continue using into adulthood. Determining whether substance use in an adolescent represents experimentation or problem use is sometimes difficult. Researchers do not consider
substance use a normal developmental process because it can interfere
with necessary developmental tasks (Schulenberg, Maggs, Steinman, &
Zucker, 2001). These tasks might include negotiating prosocial relationships with peers and family members. Substance use can interfere with
school performance and might lead to expulsion or even to arrest. In general, researchers have not developed a clearly defined set of criteria for
differentiating problem use from experimentation. However, the presence
of a set of behaviors and situational factors may help in making this determination.

Risk factors that might help you understand whether your adolescent
has a serious problem include (1) beginning to use alcohol or drugs at a
young age, (2) using frequently (weekly or daily), (3) using hard substances other than alcohol or marijuana, (4) using during school or work
hours, (5) interference with carrying out daily routines and responsibilities, and (6) parental substance use. If a youth is arrested or is suspended
from school for using drugs or alcohol, or if there is significant family conflict because of your child's use, then there is a problem.

If you notice that your child is using substances, a conversation about
his use is needed. Remember the communication techniques described in
chapter 8. Begin positively and without judgment. For example:

You: "I'm concerned about you, you seem different. Is everything okay?"

Child: "Yea, things are fine."

You: "Well, if I didn't know better, I'd think you were using drugs. I'm not
going to yell at you, I want to help."

Child: "Why do you think that I'm using drugs?!"

You: "You seem different from your normal self."

Child: "Well, maybe I am."

You (in a calm nonjudgmental tone): "What are you using?"

Child: "Pot."

You: "How often do you use pot?"

Child: "Every day."

If you determine that the problem is so severe that talk and support are not enough to help the child abstain, then outside treatment is required. You can present this to your child as follows.

You: "Lots of people struggle with this problem, and sometimes it's hard to do it by yourself. I want to help you get what you want out of life, and I worry that drugs can interfere with your goals. I'd like to set up a meeting for you to talk to someone, since it's probably too hard to talk to me about it. Okay?"

Child: "I don't want to go to a therapist."

You: "I can appreciate that, it's not always very much fun, and it's uncomfortable. But you never know, maybe it will be nice to talk to someone freely and privately. Give it a try, and then we'll talk about it later. Okay?"

Child: "Okay, I'll try it, but if I don't like them I'm not going back."

You: "Sounds good."

If the conversation does not go this smoothly, you might need to tell your child that you love him, and that going to treatment is not optional. You are the parent, and he is the child. You know what is best, and in this case there are no other options.

PARENT DOES NOT APPROVE OF CHILD'S PEER GROUP

A common parental complaint centers on the child's friends or boy-friend or girlfriend. Perhaps you perceive the friend as a negative influence on your child. Your son always seems to get in trouble when he is with this friend. Or, you observe that his attitude becomes confrontational and defiant after he returns from a day with his friend. Often, a parent's first response to this problem is to forbid the child to see the friend. But forbidding youth from seeing their peers seldom has the desired effect. A teenager who does not agree with the parent's edict might continue to meet forbidden friends at school and tell you that he is with another friend when he is actually seeing the forbidden friend.

Instead of forbidding contact, discuss your concerns with your son. You might be surprised. He might be more receptive to your concerns than you originally thought. For example, you might tell him that you fear he will not make good decisions (especially with regard to using drugs or alcohol, school behavior, and so on) when his friend pressures him to use alcohol or to skip school or to shun team sports and other extracurricular activities.

It is difficult for a child to discontinue association with a chosen peer group if he has no alternatives. Your child might be faced with losing the only support group that he knows, even if association with this group is actually self-destructive and leads to greater problems (e.g., arrest, school trouble, parent problems). Brainstorm with your son to identify alternative peer supports. That is, make a list of non-substance-using peers with whom your son might have some acquaintance. You might make a game out of it, and role-play how to approach a peer and initiate a social outing.

In addition, extracurricular programs tend to attract prosocial teenagers. Participating in an after-school activity (sports, drama, music) will increase your son's contact with new peers and is an excellent alternative to drug use and other problem behaviors. A weekend or summer job can also introduce him to other adolescents who might be more responsible than his current friends. And finally, teen Alcoholics Anonymous or Narcotics Anonymous groups allow youth to meet peers who are motivated to change their substance use and problem behaviors.

VIOLATION OF EXPECTATIONS

Even though you clearly present your expectations to your daughter, she might still slip up. She might come home after her curfew without calling you. You might receive a call from the school principal informing you that she did not attend school that day. As frustrating as these bumps in the road seem, the use of problem-solving, communication, and coping skills can still move you forward. Anger management, including being able to leave a situation and return when emotions are lower-pitched, is a prerequisite for addressing conflict and disappointment. Slips do not necessarily portend complete failure. As mentioned throughout this book, problems that were a long time in the making require time and patience to resolve.

You first must check what her slip means to you. Do you believe that her slip was a direct attack on you? Though you might feel angry and betrayed, try to remain calm. Revisit the consequences of violating behavioral expectations in a matter-of-fact manner. Let your child know your true feelings—hurt, betrayal, disappointment, fear that the relationship will disintegrate again. Let her know you still love her, but that she still has to follow the rules that you both agreed upon. Seek information from her.

How does she feel about things? Is this violation her way of telling you she needs something more or less from you? A calm discussion can repair many wounds and pave the way to renewed positive communication and interactions.

VIOLENCE: YOUTH ASSAULTS PARENT

Often, youth who assault parents have a history of being physically abused themselves. Parents do not always volunteer this information for obvious reasons—shame and fear. Youth often learn how to handle difficult situations or emotions by observing their parents in similar situations. A violent outburst by your child provides the perfect opportunity to discuss the past, present, and future—after emotions have calmed, of course. Now is the time to bring taboo topics to the table. Let your daughter know that, even though her father was abusive, she has other options to handle frustration and anger. Let her know that you believe she learned this behavior from her father, but that she must also learn other ways to handle problems. By saying this to her, you relieve her of some responsibility for her violent behavior and you give her responsibility for changing in the future. Not only is she likely to drop her defensiveness, but she will gain insight into her behavior. She might not realize that she pushed you because she saw her father push you or because her father pushed her. It seems like a simple connection to an outside observer, but it is not as obvious to those who are immersed in the situation.

All family members share responsibility for problems that occur in the family, which means that all should share in the solution. You can try the following role-play exercise, which is fun and also effective for repairing wounds. First, reintroduce the topic of conversation that led to violence, but this time use words to express feelings. State what is behind the anger (usually hurt, betrayal, frustration), then work toward a solution on which everyone can agree. You should have a plan in place prior to carrying out the role-play to prevent violence from occurring again. This plan might include appointing one person who agrees to leave the room if escalation occurs, or having a neutral party in the room during the role-play who can deescalate the conversation if it becomes overly emotional.

Your family can develop a plan for identifying situations in which escalation will occur and also develop a plan to deescalate such situations. Through effective communication, problem solving, and the use of time-outs, escalation to the point of violence will not occur. However, everyone has to work together and practice their conflict resolution skills.

If these techniques fail and your child assaults you, you might call the police. The police will probably remove her from the home. Or, she might receive temporary placement at a runaway shelter for your safety or the safety of siblings. She might receive a referral to a group home for a longer-term stay once released from juvenile detention. Sometimes violent youth are arrested, taken to the detention home, and released back to the home with the condition that they and their families receive treatment.

PARENT IS VIOLENT

If one or both adults in the home are violent, the responsibility for change lies with the adult. Children have the right to a nonabusive life and to safety within the home. If counseling or removal of the violent adult doesn't make the home safe, the child must be placed in a safe environment where her growth can be fostered.

GANG AFFILIATION

Gang involvement is common in some communities. Although many youth will deny being officially ranked into (initiated—e.g., beat up or gang raped) a particular gang, most will admit that they associate with gang members or engage in gang fighting. Some youth come from a long line of gang-involved family members—parents, siblings, even grandparents. In rare cases, the youth will state that they no longer wish to associate with other gang members. If this is the situation, then intervention focuses on working with the youth to disassociate from their gang. This includes developing relationships with non-gang-affiliated youth and practicing how to reduce affiliation with gang-involved friends.

Most youth do not have any desire to leave their gang-affiliated friends and join more prosocial groups, because they believe their gang-affiliated friends are the only friends and support they have. If your daughter is forced to leave the gang, she might feel alienated and invalidated. For this reason, voluntary disassociation is better. Her involvement and agreement to initiate the process of removing herself from the gang increases the chance of successful extraction. Increase her association with non-gang peers and her time with you. Also, increase her involvement in school-related activities. These opportunities to broaden her social support might lead her to drift away from the deviant peer group and into more prosocial groups. Some states have gang intervention counselors who can also assist in this process. A call to your state's Child, Youth and Family Department can point you in the right direction.

YOUTH ARRESTED FOR SHOPLIFTING, DRUGS, OR OTHER CRIME

Nothing turns a good day bad like a call from the juvenile detention center informing you that your daughter has been arrested.

If your child is arrested for the first time for a misdemeanor, the judge will likely release her into your custody with the mandate that she (or the entire family) attend therapy. She might receive a time waiver, which is an agreement by the court to keep the transgression off her record if she stays within the law for a specified period of time.

Some youth who run away from home have had prior contact with the juvenile justice system and might be on probation. Incarceration is the usual outcome for a youth with multiple prior offenses. This experience could frighten a child who has never stayed overnight in a detention setting enough to stay out of trouble in the future.

A brush with the law is not necessarily an indication that your child will engage in a lifetime of crime. Many adolescents will never again have trouble with the police. Your approach to this situation should again start with clear, nonblaming communication that identifies expectations and the consequences of not meeting these expectations. Share your feelings, and ask your child to share hers. She might feel that she destroyed any chance of building a relationship with you. She might fear that you will never trust her again. You and she can rebuild the relationship by working out a plan for her to rebuild the trust that was lost. Such a plan should include concrete and specific behaviors. Clearly identify what she needs to do in order to rebuild your trust and confidence in her. The plan might include the completion of extra chores, returning one hour earlier than the normal curfew, completing homework prior to dinnertime every evening, and so on.

PREGNANCY

In the University of New Mexico's Runaway and Homeless Youth Program, 30 percent of adolescent runaways who have been through the program have children, were pregnant at the intake evaluation, or became pregnant during the course of the 18-month period in which we tracked them. Pregnancy creates myriad issues for the family and adolescent to work out. You will likely find that your daughter's reaction to her pregnancy is mixed. She might feel excited at the prospect of creating a human life and raising a child of her own. She might feel terrified: "How can I care for my child and finish school? Will my parents support me?" Your reaction might range from anger to irritation to confusion to excitement.

You might wonder if you are now expected to raise and support another child—one you did not plan.

You might need to help your daughter identify the additional requirements that will be placed upon her as a new mother. This includes helping her evaluate her living, financial, and health care situation. If she is an active drug or alcohol user, focus on her substance use immediately. If needed, you or she must make an appointment to receive an intensive intervention that might include either inpatient care or detoxification from alcohol or drugs. If intensive intervention is not needed, outpatient care may provide enough support so that the problem is addressed. Most programs put pregnant mothers at the top of their waiting lists, so identify her as such. The treatment program should educate her about the effects of alcohol, tobacco, and other drug use on the developing fetus. Arrange prenatal care for her, and transport and accompany her to her appointments if you feel comfortable with that, or if she needs you.

The decision to abort a child involves religious, social, economic, and personal factors. Deciding what is right for you and your family is not always easy. Outside guidance and assistance is available through many programs, including Planned Parenthood and public health agencies.

If your son is an expectant father, consider inviting his pregnant girlfriend to a family dinner. Talk with your son and his girlfriend about their plans for raising the child and how each will work to provide a stable environment for the child while pursuing their own educational or career goals. Issues for negotiation may include living arrangements for the couple. Do they wish to live together, and what would your expectations be for such an arrangement? Your pregnant daughter or your expecting son might need to know how much financial support you will be willing to provide, so prepare yourself for that question.

YOUTH DIAGNOSED WITH A SEXUALLY TRANSMITTED DISEASE (STD)

Research from the University of New Mexico's Runaway and Homeless Youth Program indicates that over 60 percent of youth report lack of consistent condom use, and that the majority were sexually active and had multiple sexual partners in the prior 12 months (Slesnick, 2003). If your child is afraid and ashamed, you may never know that she suffers from an STD. Alternatively, you and she might have a very open relationship, and she will tell you. She might not know what to do and might need your support and comfort. Admonishment, even though you may feel disgusted, angry, or disappointed, will not help her or you.

Prevention work is important. Even though she already contracted an STD, she is still at risk for contracting another STD. In addition, she must learn that her STD is transmittable to other sexual partners. This highlights the need to use condoms if sexual activity will continue. Female or male condom use is necessary for both oral sex and intercourse.

In many states, youth are able to receive STD testing and treatment without guardian consent. However, the counselor should discuss the youth's concerns about informing her guardian about her STD. Youth may fear further rejection or judgment that might compound the shame they already experience. In any case, the therapist can coordinate medical care and educate the youth about the particular STD that they have contracted. If you cannot discuss sexual matters with your child, send her to an agency or to a counselor who has experience and is comfortable with discussing the topic.

CONCLUSION: AND WHAT NOW?

Every day we are learning more about kids who run away, what their families are like, and what happens when they leave home. But there are still holes in our knowledge. For instance, we do not know why some kids run away and others from similar home environments do not. We do not yet know how those who go to shelters or couch surf are different from those who go straight to the streets. Many youth who reside at a runaway shelter eventually return home, but a certain proportion of them run away again. Are those the youth who turn to the streets and become chronically homeless? Or are street-living youth completely different from those who run away to shelters? How do we identify youth who are on their way to becoming street-living youth or homeless adults? How or when do youth become integrated back into the mainstream culture on their own? What does an adult who ran away as an adolescent look like, and how can we predict which former runaways will become successful adults and which will not? How do we predict problematic versus adaptive running away? How can we best intervene, since there are no published treatment outcome studies available to guide our intervention? Though great strides have been made, research on this population, including intervention strategies, is still in its infancy.

Certainly, the goal of some researchers is eventually to prevent homelessness among youth. In order to prevent this problem, we need more answers to the above questions. It is likely that, even with prevention policies and procedures in place, societies will still struggle with homelessness. A flu shot is no guarantee that you will not get the flu. So even though prevention is the goal of many, we will always need to learn how to re-integrate a homeless child into his home or into mainstream society.

Part II provides strategies that might prove useful to parents who are dealing with a runaway. Parents who read this book can take some comfort in knowing that millions of other families are going through, or have gone through, a similar situation. Other families have experienced some of the same feelings and thoughts, and have had similar defeats and victories in handling the situation. The reaction of family members to having a run-away child will vary depending upon the relationship between family members. Some family members might be distraught, while others might feel guilty about their relief in having the child out of the home. Whatever the case may be, the guidance in Part II is designed to help the family work toward a mutually rewarding relationship with the runaway child. And in the next decade, researchers and clinicians will likely learn more strategies to serve runaway youth and their families. Treatment intervention manuals may become available, and struggling parents and children will feel greater support from the community. Given the magnitude and the impact that homelessness has on individuals and families, as well as its cost to society, this problem should be an important focus of research and funding efforts.

The diversity of characteristics of runaways and their families is great, as is the diversity of outcomes for those who run away and for the parents of runaways. Although some families endure great pain, many renew and strengthen bonds that were broken because of the crisis. Like a phoenix rising from the ashes, some families gain strength from the lessons they learned and the losses they might have experienced. What keeps a family going in the face of its struggle? Love for a child or a parent can forgive some of the biggest transgressions. Who knows more about unconditional love than a parent for a child and a child for a parent?

Other times, the lives of families with runaways do not change for the better. In some cases, the child leaves and does not return for extended peri-ods of time, and the relationship continues to disintegrate into adulthood. But the child might still go on to have a successful and happy life apart from his family of origin. Take, for example, Dan, who looks back on his life as a runaway 20 years ago. Dan lived on and off with his parents as an adolescent, and never experienced long periods of stability or emotional repair. Rejection and hurt dominated the relationship with his parents.

> My dad was an authority figure, not a father figure. Until I turned 10 years
> old, I was afraid of him—I suppose because I associated him with punish-

ment. He spanked me with a belt or paddle, and there was nothing else to balance out the punishment. He spanked the hell out of me one time because I knocked over a bucket of paint. Since he was always working, I didn't see him much and we didn't do a lot together. He's not a monster or anything like that. He was a funny guy, and sometimes he did funny stuff. I really tried to be good, so I didn't get punished all of the time. But my brother and I both got in trouble if one of us didn't confess to doing something wrong.

When I was a kid, I loved my mom very much, I had a real close relationship with her. I spent a lot of time with her and I bet I kissed her 100 times a day. I wanted to be close to her—she was beautiful. One day we were in the basement, I went to give her a kiss and she pushed me away. In later years she told me that she had favored me for a long time and it was my brother's turn to be favored. Then our relationship became strained and she became standoffish all of sudden. From that point on, the deck was stacked against me, they weren't friendly towards me and I was always in a defensive posture. It felt like they were ready to have their own life, like they were done raising children.

Since I never did a lot with my dad or my mom, it seemed like we just coexisted, but with a lot a rules placed on me. It was not a great family atmosphere in my opinion. One thing that started the strain with my parents was my relationship with my girlfriend. My mother didn't want me to see her anymore, and I didn't like that because my mom and my dad weren't really involved in my life except to make rules. They said "If you want to make your own rules, you can go live somewhere else." So I grabbed a few things and went to live at my best friend's house for a while. That was when I was 15 years old.

In Dan's adult years, he continues to struggle with his relationship with his mother and father.

My life was really hard. When I was a kid, my parents sent me to counseling to straighten *ME* out. But I think it's always been like that. . . . *I* have the problem, *I'm* the one with some kind of mental disease, and *I* have been the catalyst of all the problems for them. I think that's how they feel.

I don't hate them or anything. When my mom tells me she loves me, I don't believe it because I don't believe she knows what that means. I don't believe she has respect for me to this day. I had an affair a year back, it's a painful subject that I don't like to talk about. But I did make choices after the affair because I really love my wife and I wanted to stay with her. Definitely I want to be with my wife and daughter. This is the best family I've ever known even with the problems we've had.

My mom's not happy with the way I turned out. That's just what I feel. The whole thing is very sad. The most sad is that the things I remember, like the fights, they don't remember, or they say it's water under the bridge. I have always apologized for what I said in the past. All my mother would have to say is "I'm sorry" or "I remember what happened during that fight and that was wrong." She doesn't even have to take blame for it. That's how we move past things.

My parents would say that I didn't come with a manual. I don't blame them for everything. I just don't want them to blame me for the way they perceive me, because that's their perception. There are a lot of people who would argue that I have more character than they think. I don't think that myself. I know I'm judgmental and hypercritical of other people and complain a lot about a myriad of subjects and circumstances. But I work on those things. One thing I remember from our history lessons in school is that Ben Franklin made a list each day about things that he could do better. So I try to make a mental list of things I could do better, and I try to make amends for things that I have done.

I'm 35 now, and when I have nothing to do with them, I always seem to make out better and adjust to whatever the circumstances are. I have friends. They all know that I'm a person who goes that extra mile for them and that I will do whatever I can to help them have a good life. I do that for my wife, and for my daughter.

His childhood experience with his parents helps him with his newly formed family. So in this case, even though his relationship with his parents was not repaired when he was a child or even an adult, he vowed to have a different relationship with his own child, and he has not repeated the same patterns with her.

I got married in 1993, and that was a turning point in my life. It was a slow turning point—I was pretty young, 25, but now I'm very happy because my wife doesn't give me a free pass on anything. She is my number-one friend first. She makes comments that I don't like sometimes, but it causes me to examine myself. My daughter is 10 years old now. She's an angel, even if she does stuff I don't like. I believe that there's a protective instinct for your children and that you naturally want to do things for them. I don't feel that my parents had that interest in me like I have in my daughter.

I'm not always a perfect person or the best dad, but I do make an attempt to do my best and treat people the best. I asked my daughter if I was the best dad in the world, and she said four and a quarter out of seven days. At first I thought it would be better if she said I was the best dad seven out of seven days, but percentage-wise four and a quarter out of seven is 60 percent, and that's pretty good if someone thinks you're the best daddy 60 percent of the time.

Sometimes I get upset, and my wife has to remind me that I'm not my father. My parents came close to making me the way they are. My dad yelled at us, enraged, and I think that leaves an imprint on you; and if you're not conscious of it when you're older, you start doing the same thing. Luckily, I put the brakes on it, and if I realize that I'm not acting up to par, I can apologize to my daughter and say "Your Dad is a grump. I shouldn't have been that hard on you, and I was wrong." I have to credit my best friend's family for that. Being around their family influenced me. They had a hand in molding my character to own up to things and be good to other people.

I was enamored with my first girlfriend because her family cared at a level I didn't have with my family, and I never knew that level. My in-laws are that way too. There will never be a family reunion for my family; it was dysfunctional from the get-go. My brother chose one way to deal with it and I chose another. I'm far too sensitive to be a member of that family. Now, when I hack away at my parents verbally, it's because I think they taught me to do that. I'd never talk to my mom that way if there were some kind of bond there.

In this case, most people would agree that Dan and his parents did not have a happy ending to the crises in adolescence. However, 20 years later he is married, with a young daughter, and he finally has the family he always wished for. He works hard to not repeat the mistakes he felt his parents made. When he makes mistakes, he accepts responsibility for them, learns, and works harder to do better next time. He does not blame or deny his part in the problem. His will to love and be loved carries him through his pain. And now, he has his own family that loves him and that he in turn cherishes. He is no longer homeless; he is not in prison or addicted to drugs; and he is still alive. His struggle has been rewarded.

Some children return home to their families after living with others, living in hotels, prostituting, or couch surfing. The issues that led to running away were addressed, and the family reunited stronger from having experienced the near collapse of their relationships. These families are often characterized by an intense desire not to let their relationships die. Their will to succeed forced a successful resolution.

I don't want him to live on the streets. He can get killed; he won't be able to finish school; and I miss him...this just can't happen. I'll do whatever it takes to get him back home. I know we can work things out, he is still my son. I made mistakes and he made mistakes but we can get through this, I know we can.

This father is at the brink of losing his child. He has not seen his son in weeks and does not know if he is okay. He will do anything to get his son back. I have seen parents search the streets for a son or daughter, crying hysterically, regretting the things that they said or did to their child. I have seen terror in the eyes of parents who think that they might never see their son or daughter again. I have watched the anger from all past insults give way to raw desperation. That desperation drives parents' will to do anything to have their child back home. For them, there are no other options.

When I sit with a parent like this I know that when we find his son, things will work out. Though the father implores me to help him and his son, I know that I am insignificant compared to what has already happened. The father is committed to getting his son back and making changes in the family. His son is returning home. My role is only to facilitate the process. For many families, the child returns home; and although the family struggles with new ways of talking and new ways of handling frustration, the bond of love and family prevails.

And there can be partial hard-won successes, too. I worked with a single mother and her daughter. At first, neither mother nor daughter would discuss any problems they had experienced, even though the daughter had lived on her own for several months in an abandoned building, surviving by dealing drugs and shoplifting. Finally, the emotional wall between them began to crumble, and they talked about their struggles with each other. Feelings and frustrations were openly shared, and misunderstandings were corrected. We worked hard. The daughter returned home, and she stayed home for nearly one year. I later heard that she had gotten pregnant at age 17, and moved out of the home. She moved into a program that served teenage mothers, where she was able to go to school and receive job training with the support of the program staff. She and her mother were still communicating, and she said she still feels close to her mother. She had plans to continue with school after she finished high school. And she said several times, "I need to settle down for my daughter. She depends on me, and I'm going to always be there for her. I'm not going to let anyone hurt my baby."

I also work with adolescents who do not reunite with their parents. Street-living youth who have been abandoned by their parents, or who suffered extreme abuse at their parents' hands, often do not return home. Early on in my work with these kids, I wondered what would happen to them. How would they get through life without having the guidance and anchors that many of us have? I watch their drive to be loved, to love, and to know that someone else understands them. Many of these kids protect other kids who live on the streets. They emphatically state that they want to finish school so that they can help others like them, or vow that they will never treat their own children the way they were treated. Their painful experience is the driving force that carries them through their lives. A history of suffering does not preclude their continued search and striving for a life of peace, love, and acceptance.

REFERENCES

Able-Peterson, T. (1989). *The most forgotten adolescents.* Presentation at conference on Treatment of Adolescents with Alcohol, Drug Abuse, and Mental Health Problem, Alexandria, VA.

Alexander, J. F., & Parsons, B. V. (1982). *Functional family therapy: Principles and procedures.* Carmel, CA: Brooks/Cole.

Anderson, J. E., Freese, T. E., & Pennbridge, J. N. (1994). Sexual risk behavior and condom use among street youth in Hollywood. *Family Planning Perspectives, 26,* 22–25.

Athey, J. L. (1989). *Pregnancy and childbearing among homeless adolescents: Report of a workshop, October 16–17, 1989, Rockville, MD.* Pittsburgh, PA: University of Pittsburgh.

Athey, J. L. (1995). HIV infection and homeless adolescents. In E. R. Bethel (Ed.), *AIDS: Reading on a global crisis* (pp. 354–364). Needham Heights, MA: Allyn and Bacon.

Axthelm, P. (1988, 25 April). Somebody else's kids. *Newsweek,* 64–68.

Bahr, S. J., Hawks, R. D., & Wang, G. (1993). Family and religious influences on adolescent substance abuse. *Youth and Society, 24*(4), 443–465.

Baron, S. W., & Hartnagel, T. F. (1998). Street youth and criminal violence. *Journal of Research in Crime and Delinquency, 35* (2), 166–192.

Barth, R. P. (1990). Theories guiding home-based intensive family preservation services. In J. K. Whittaker, J. Kinney, E. M. Tracy, & C. Booth (Eds.), *Reaching high risk families: Intensive family preservation services in human services* (pp. 89–112). New York: Aldine.

Booth, R. E., & Zhang, Y. (1997). Conduct disorder and HIV risk behaviors among runaway and homeless adolescents. *Drug and Alcohol Dependence, 48,* 69–76.

Burbach, D. J., & Borduin, C. M. (1986). Parent-child relations and the etiology of depression: A review of methods and findings. *Clinical Psychology Review, 6*(2), 133–153.

Carmen, E. H., & Rieker, P. P. (1989). A psychosocial model of the victim-to-patient process. *Psychiatric Clinics of North America, 12,* 431–443.

Cauce, A. M., Morgan, C. J., Wagner, V., Moore, E., Sy, J., Wurzbacher, K., Weeden, K., Tomlin, S., & Blanchard, T. (1994). Effectiveness of intensive case management for homeless adolescents: Results of a 3-month follow-up. Special series: Center for Mental Health Services Research Projects. *Journal of Emotional and Behavioral Disorders, 2,* 219–227.

Centers for Disease Control. (1993). *HIV/AIDS surveillance report* (Year-end edition). Atlanta, GA: Author.

Coyne, J. C. (1976). Toward an interactional description of depression. *Psychiatry, 39,* 28–40.

Cunningham, R. M., Stiffman, A. R., & Dore, P. (1994). The association of physical & sexual abuse with HIV risk behaviors in adolescence and young adulthood: Implications for public health. *Child Abuse and Neglect, 18* (3), 233–245.

Daley, S. (1988, November 14). New York City street youth: Living in the shadow of AIDS. *The New York Times,* B1, B4.

Deisher, R. W., Farrow, J. A., Hope, K., & Litchfield, C. (1989). The pregnant adolescent prostitute. *American Journal of Diseases of Children, 143,* 1162–1165.

De Rosa, C. J., Montgomery, S. B., Kipke, M. D., Iverson, E., Ma, J. L., & Unger, J. B. (1999). Service utilization among homeless and runaway youth in Los Angeles, California: Rates and reasons. *Journal of Adolescent Health, 24,* 449–458.

Dishion, T. J., Capaldi, D., Spracklen, K. M., & Li, F. (1995). Peer ecology of male adolescent drug use. *Development & Psychopathology Special Issue, 7*(4), 803–824.

Dishion, T. J., Patterson, G. R., & Reid, J. R. (1988). *Parent and peer factors associated with drug sampling in early adolescence: Implications for treatment.* (NIDA Research Monograph, 77, 69–93).

Earls, F. (1989). Studying adolescent suicidal ideation and behavior in primary care settings. *Suicide and Life-Threatening Behaviors, 19,* 99–119.

Elliott, D. S. (1994). Serious violent offenders: Onset, developmental course, and termination. *Criminology, 32,* 1–22.

English, A. (1999). Health care for the adolescent alone: A legal landscape. In J. Blustein, C. Levine, & N. N. Subler (Eds.), *The adolescent alone* (pp. 78–99). Cambridge, UK: Cambridge University Press.

Fagan, J. A., Piper, E. S., & Moore, M. (1986). Violent delinquents and urban youths. *Criminology, 24,* 439–471.

Famularo, R., Kinscherff, R., Fenton, T., & Bolduc, S. M. (1990). Child maltreatment histories among runaway and delinquent children. *Clinical Pediatrics, 29,* 713–718.

Feldman, L. H. (1991). Evaluating the impact of intensive family preservation services in New Jersey. In K. Wells & D. A. Biegel (Eds.), *Family preservation services: Research and evaluation* (pp. 47–71). Newbury Park, CA: Sage.

Finkelhor, D., Hotaling, G., & Sedlak, A. (1990). *Missing, abducted, runaway and thrownaway children in America: First report.* Washington, DC: U.S. Department of Justice, Office of Juvenile Justice and Delinquency Prevention.

Forehand, R., Miller, K. S., Dutra, R., & Chance, M. W. (1997). Role of parenting in adolescent deviant behavior: Replication across and within two ethnic groups. *Journal of Consulting and Clinical Psychology, 65,* 1036–1041.

Garinger, T., Brant, D., & Brant, V. (1976). Preserving parents' and children's rights. In G. P. Koocher (Ed.), *Children's rights and the mental health professions* (pp. 53–81). New York: John Wiley & Sons.

General Accounting Office. (1989). *Homelessness: Homeless and runaway youth receiving services at federally funded shelters* (GAO Publication No. HRD-90-45). Washington, DC: Author.

Goodman, J. K. (1972). Preventing the causes of drug abuse. *Journal of Drug Education, 2,* 263–268.

Gottman, J. M., & Levenson, R. W. (2002). Couples and family research—A two-factor model for predicting when a couple will divorce: Exploratory analyses using 14-year longitudinal data. *Family Process, 41,* 83–94.

Gould, P. (1993). The slow plague: A geography of the AIDS pandemic. Cambridge, MA: Blackwell.

Grigsby, R. K. (1992). Mental health consultation at the youth shelter: An ethnographic approach. *Child & Youth Care Forum, 21,* 247–261.

Haerian, M. (1998). Foster care. In H. S. Ghuman, & R. M. Sarles (Eds.), *Handbook of child and adolescent outpatient, day treatment and community psychiatry* (pp. 377–384). Philadelphia, PA: Brunner-Mazel.

Hagan, J., & McCarthy, B. (1992). Streetlife and delinquency. *British Journal of Sociology, 43,* 533–561.

Henggeler, S. W., Borduin, C. M., Melton, G. B., Mann, B. J., Smith L. A., Hall, J. A., Cone, L., & Fucci, B. R. (1991). Effects of multisystemic therapy on drug use and abuse in serious juvenile offenders: A progress report from two outcome studies. *Family Dynamics of Addiction Quarterly, 1,* 40–51.

Herdt, G. (1989). Introduction: Gay and lesbian youth, emergent identities, and cultural scenes at home and abroad. *Journal of Homosexuality, Special Issue, 17,* 1–42.

Herman, D. B., Struening, E. L., & Barrow, S. M. (1993). Self-assessed need for mental health services among homeless adults. *Hospital and Community Psychiatry, 44* (12), 1181–1183.

Hirsch, B. J., Moos, R. H., & Reischl, T. M. (1985). Psychosocial adjustment of adolescent children of a depressed, arthritic, or normal parent. *Journal of Abnormal Psychology, 94,* 154–164.

Humm, A. (1990). *Out of the shadows: Building an agenda and strategies for prevention of HIV/AIDS in street and homeless youth.* New York: Hetrick Martin Institute.

James, S. (1978). Treatment of homosexuality: II. Superiority of desensitization/arousal as compared with anticipatory avoidance conditioning: Results of a controlled trial. *Behavior Therapy, 9,* 28–36.

Jensen, P. S., Bhatara, V. S., Vitiello, B., Hoagwood, K., Feil, M., & Burke, L. B. (1999). Psychoactive medication prescribing practices for U.S. children: Gaps between research and clinical practice. *Journal of the American Academy of Child and Adolescent Psychiatry, 38,* 557–565.

Jessor, R., & Jessor, S. L. (1977). The social-psychological framework. In R. Jessor & S. L. Jessor (Eds.), *Problem behavior and psychosocial development: A longitudinal study of youth* (pp. 17–42). New York: Academic Press.

Johnson, T. P., Aschkenasy, J. R., Herbers, M. R., & Gillenwater, S. A. (1996). Self-reported risk factors for AIDS among homeless youth. *AIDS Education and Prevention, 8,* 308–322.

Kaliski, E. M., Rubinson, L., Lawrence, L., & Levy, S. R. (1990). AIDS, runaways, and self-efficacy. *Family and Community Health, 13,* 60–67.

Kelly, J. T. (1985). Trauma: With the example of San Francisco's shelter programs. In P. W. Brickner, L. K. Scharer, B. Conanan, A. Elvy, & M. Savarese (Eds.), *Health care of homeless people.* New York: Springer.

Kinney, J., Haapala, D., Madsen, B., & Fleming, T. (1977). Homebuilders: Keeping families together. *Journal of Counseling and Consulting Psychology, 14,* 209–213.

Kipke, M. D., Montgomery, S. B., & MacKenzie, R. (1993). Substance use among youth seen at a community-based health clinic. *Journal of Adolescent Health, 14,* 289–294.

Kipke, M. D., Montgomery, S. B., Simon, T. R., & Iverson, E. F. (1997). Substance abuse disorders among runaways and homeless youth. *Substance Use and Misuse, 32,* 969–986.

Kipke, M. D., Simon, T. R., Montgomery, S. B., Unger, J. B., & Iverson, E. F. (1997). Homeless youth and their exposure to and involvement in violence while living on the streets. *Journal of Adolescent Health, 20,* 360–367.

Klein, J. D., Woods, A. H., Wilson, K. M., Prospero, M., Greene, J., & Ringwalt, C. (2000). Homeless and runaway youths' access to health care. *Journal of Adolescent Health, 27,* 331–339.

Koopman, C., Rosario, M., & Rotheram-Borus, M. J. (1994). Alcohol and drug use and sexual behaviors placing runaways at risk for HIV infection. *Addictive Behaviors, 19,* 95–103.

Kral, A. H., Molnar, B. E., Booth, R. E., & Watters, J. K. (1997). Prevalence of sexual risk behavior and substance use among runaway and homeless adolescent in San Francisco, Denver and New York City. *International Journal of STDs & AIDS, 8,* 109–117.

Kruks, G. (1991). Gay and lesbian homeless/street youth: Special issues and concerns. *Journal of Adolescent Health, 12,* 515–518.

Kufeldt, K., Durieux, M., Nimmo, M., & McDonald, M. (1992). Providing shelter for street youth: Are we reaching those in need? *Child Abuse and Neglect, 16,* 187–199.

Kufeldt, K., & Nimmo, M. (1987). Youth on the street: Abuse and neglect in the eighties. *Child Abuse and Neglect, 11,* 531–543.

Kurtz, P. D., Jarvis, S. V., & Kurtz, G. L. (1991). Problems of homeless youths: Empirical findings and human services issues. *Social Work, 36,* 309–314.

Kurtz, P. D., Kurtz, G. L., & Jarvis, G. L. (1991). Problems of maltreated runaway youth. *Adolescence, 26,* 543–555.

Marshall, E. J., & Bhugra, D. (1996). Services for the mentally ill homeless. In D. Bhugra (Ed.), *Homelessness and mental health* (pp. 99–109). Cambridge, UK: Cambridge University Press.

McCarthy, B., & Hagan, J. (1992). Surviving the street: The experiences of homeless youth. *Journal of Adolescent Research, 7,* 412–430.

McMillen, J. C., & Tucker, J. (1999). The status of older adolescents at exit from out-of-home care. *Child Welfare, 78,* 339–360.

Melton, G. B., Lyons, P. M., & Spaulding, W. J. (1998). *No place to go: The civil commitment of minors.* Lincoln, NE: The University of Nebraska Press.

Miller, H. G., Turner, C. F., & Moses, L. E. (1990). *AIDS: The second decade.* Washington, DC: National Academy Press.

Miller, W. R., Brown, J. M., Simpson, T. L., Handmaker, N. S., Bien, T. H., Luckie, L. F., Montgomery, H. A., Hester, R. K., & Tonigan, J. S. (1995). What works? A methodological analysis of the alcohol treatment outcome literature. In R. K. Hester & W. R. Miller (Eds.), *Handbook of alcoholism treatment approaches* (2nd ed., pp. 12–44). Needham Heights, MA: Allyn & Bacon.

Minuchin, S., & Nichols, M. P. (1998). *Family healing.* New York: Free Press.

Molnar, B. E., Shade, S. B., Kral, A. H., Booth, R. E., & Watters, J. K. (1998). Suicidal behavior and sexual/physical abuse among street youth. *Child Abuse and Neglect, 22,* 213–222.

Morrissette, P. (1992). Engagement strategies with reluctant homeless young people. *Psychotherapy, 29,* 447–451.

Mundy, P., Robertson, M., Robertson, J., & Greenblatt, M. (1990). The prevalence of psychotic symptoms in homeless adolescents. *Journal of the American Academy of Child and Adolescent Psychiatry, 29,* 724–731.

Munro, E. (1999). Common errors of reasoning in child protection work. *Child Abuse and Neglect, 23,* 745–758.

Myers, M. G., Brown, S. A., & Mott, M. A. (1993). Coping as a predictor of adolescent substance abuse treatment outcome. *Journal of Substance Abuse, 5,* 15–29.

National Clearinghouse on Child Abuse and Neglect (2003). *Child maltreatment 2001: Summary of key findings.* Washington, DC: Author.

National Network of Runaway and Youth Services. (1991). *To whom do they belong? Runaway, homeless and other youth in high-risk situations in the 1990s.* Washington, DC: Author.

Nelson, K. (1994). Innovative delivery models in social services. *Journal of Clinical Child Psychology, 23,* 26–31.

Nelson, K. E., & Landsman, M. J. (1992). *Alternative models of family preservation: Family-based services in context.* Springfield, IL: Thomas.

Olson, D. H. (1993). Circumplex model of marital and family systems: Assessing family functioning. In W. Froma (Ed.), *Normal family processes* (pp. 104–137). New York: Guilford Press.

Patterson, G. R. (1975). *Families: Applications of social learning to family life.* Champaign, IL: Research Press.

Patterson, G. R., & Stouthamer-Loeber, M. (1984). The correlation of family management practices and delinquency. *Child Development, 55,* 1299–1307.

Pedersen, W., & Aas, H. (1995). Full for forste gange—En longitudinell Studie [Drunk for the first time—A Longitudinal Study]. *Nord. Alkohol Tidskr, 12* (3), 121–131.

Pennbridge, J. N., Freese, T. E., & MacKenzie, R. G. (1992). High-risk behaviors among male street youth in Hollywood, California. *AIDS Education and Prevention* (Fall Suppl.), 24–33.

Piaget, J. (1972). Intellectual evolution from adolescence to adulthood. *Human Development, 15,* 1–12.

Post, P., & McCoard, D. (1994). Needs and self-concept of runaway adolescents. *The School Counselor, 41,* 212–219.

Ringwalt, C. L., Greene, J. M., & Robertson, M. J. (1998). Familial backgrounds and risk behaviors of youth with thrownaway experiences. *Journal of Adolescence, 21,* 241–252.

Robertson, M. (1989). *Homeless youth in Hollywood: Patterns of alcohol use: A report of the National Institute on Alcohol Abuse and Alcoholism.* Berkeley, CA: Alcohol Research Group, School of Public Health, University of Southern California.

Rohr, M. E., & James, R. (1994). Runaways: Some suggestions for prevention, coordinating services, and expediting the reentry process. *The School Counselor, 42,* 40–47.

Rose, R. J. (1998). A developmental behavioral-genetic perspective on alcoholism risk. *Alcohol Health and Research World, 22,* 131–143.

Rotheram-Borus, M. J. (1991, June 17). Testimony at hearing, The risky business of adolescence: How to help teens stay safe. Select Committee on Children, Youth and Families, U.S. House of Representatives, Washington, DC.

Rotheram-Borus, M. J. (1993). Suicidal behavior and risk factors among runaway youths. *American Journal of Psychiatry, 150,* 103–107.

Rotheram-Borus, M. J., Feldman, J., Rosario, M., & Dunne, E. (1994). Preventing HIV among runaways: Victims and victimization. In R.J. DiClemente & J. L. Peterson (Eds.), *Troubled adolescents and HIV infections.* Washington, DC: Georgetown University Child Development Center.

Rotheram-Borus, M. J., Koopman, C., & Bradley, J. S. (1989). Barriers to successful AIDS prevention programs with runaway youth. In J. O. Woodruff, D. Doherty, & J. G. Athey (Eds.), *Troubled adolescents and HIV infections.* Washington, DC: Georgetown University Child Development Center.

Rotheram-Borus, M. J., Koopman, C., Haignere, C., & Davies, M. (1991). Reducing HIV sexual risk behaviors among runaway adolescents. *Journal of the American Medical Association, 266,* 1237–1241.

Rotheram-Borus, M. J., Meyer-Bahlburg, H. F. L., Koopman, C., Rosario, M., Exner, T. M., Henderson, R., Matthieu, M., & Gruen, R. S. (1992). Lifetime sexual behaviors among runaway males and females. *Journal of Sex Research, 29,* 15–29.

Safren, S. A., & Heimberg, R. G. (1999). Depression, hopelessness, suicidality, and related factors in sexual minority and heterosexual adolescents. *Journal of Consulting and Clinical Psychology, 67,* 859–866.

Savin-Williams, R. C. (1994). Verbal and physical abuse as stressors in the lives of lesbian, gay male, and bisexual youths: Associations with school problems, running away, substance abuse, prostitution, and suicide. *Journal of Consulting and Clinical Psychology, 62,* 261–269.

Schneider, S. G., Farberow, N. L., & Kruks, G. N. (1989). Suicidal behavior in adolescent and young adult gay men. *Suicide and Life-Threatening Behavior, 19,* 381–394.

Schulenberg, J., Maggs, J. L., Steinman, K. J., & Zucker, R. A. (2001). Development matters: Taking the long view on substance abuse etiology and intervention during adolescence. In P. M. Monti, S. M. Colby, & T. O'Leary (Eds.), *Adolescents, alcohol and substance abuse* (pp. 19–57). New York: Guilford.

Schweitzer, R. D., & Hier, S. J. (1993). Psychological maladjustment among homeless adolescents. *Australian and New Zealand Journal of Psychiatry, 27,* 275–280.

Seattle Department of Human Resources. (1988). *Report on gay and lesbian youth in Seattle.* Seattle, WA: Commission on Children and Youth.

Shaffer, D., & Caton, C. L. M. (1984). *Runaway and homeless youth in New York City.* A report to the Ittleson Foundation, New York City.

Shalwitz, J. C., Goulart, M., Dunnigan, K., & Flannery, D. (1990). *Prevalence of sexually transmitted diseases (STDs) and HIV in a homeless youth medical clinic in San Francisco.* Paper presented at the VI International AIDS Conference, San Francisco.

Sherman, D. J. (1992). The neglected health care needs of street youth. *Public Health Reports, 107,* 433–440.

Sibthorpe, B., Drinkwater, J., Gardner, K., & Bammer, G. (1995). Drug use, binge drinking, and attempted suicide among homeless and potentially homeless youth. *Australian and New Zealand Journal of Psychiatry, 29,* 248–256.

Slesnick, N. (2003). *Treatment Manual: Ecologically-Based Family Therapy for Substance Abusing Runaway Youth.* Unpublished manuscript.

Slesnick, N., & Meade, M. (2001). System youth: A subgroup of substance-abusing homeless adolescents. *Journal of Substance Abuse, 13,* 367–384.

Slesnick, N., Meade, M., & Tonigan, J. S. (2001). Relationship between service utilization and runaway youths' alcohol and other drug use. *Alcoholism Treatment Quarterly, 19,* 19–29.

Slesnick, N., Meyers, R. J., Meade, M., & Segelken, D. H. (2000). Bleak and hopeless no more: Engagement of reluctant substance abusing runaway youth and their families. *Journal of Substance Abuse Treatment, 19,* 215–222.

Slesnick, N., Vasquez, C., & Bittinger, J. (2002). Family functioning: Substance use and related problem behaviors: Hispanic vs. Anglo runaway youths. *Journal of Ethnicity in Substance Abuse, 1* (4), 83–102.

Smart, R. G., & Adlaf, E. M. (1991). Substance use and problems among Toronto's street youth. *British Journal of Addiction, 86,* 999–1010.

Smart, R. G., & Ogborne, A. C. (1994). Street youth in substance abuse treatment: Characteristics and treatment compliance. *Adolescence, 29,* 733–745.

Smith, K., & Crawford, S. (1986). Suicidal behavior among abnormal high school students. *Suicide and Life-Threatening Behavior, 19,* 313–325.

St. Lawrence, J. S. (1993). African-American adolescents' knowledge, health-related attitudes, sexual behavior, and contraceptive decisions: Implications for the prevention of adolescent HIV infection. *Journal of Consulting and Clinical Psychology, 61,* 104–112.

Stricof, R. L., Kennedy, J. T., Nattell, T. C., Weisfuse, I. B., & Novick, L. F. (1991). HIV-seroprevalence in a facility for runaway and homeless adolescents. *American Journal of Public Health, 81,* 50–53.

Sullivan, T. R. (1994). Obstacles to effective child welfare service with gay and lesbian youths. *Child Welfare, 73* (4), 291–304.

Teare, J. F., Furst, D. W., Peterson, R. W., & Authier, K. (1992). Family reunification following shelter placement: Child, family, and program correlates. *American Journal of Orthopsychiatry, 62,* 142–146.

Teare, J. F., Peterson, R. W., Furst, D., Authier, K., Baker, G., & Daly, D. L. (1994). Treatment implementation in a short-term emergency shelter program. *Child Welfare, 123,* 271–283.

Thomas, A. M., & Forehand, R. (1991). The relationship between paternal depressive mood and early adolescent functioning. *Journal of Family Psychology, 4,* 260–271.

Unger, J. B., Kipke, M. D., Simon, T. R., Montgomery, S. B., & Johnson, C. J. (1997). Homeless youths and young adults in Los Angeles: Prevalence of mental health and substance abuse disorders. *American Journal of Community Psychology, 25,* 371–394.

U.S. Department of Health and Human Services. (1999a). *Code of Federal Regulations, Title 45, Volume 4, Part 1351: Runaway and Homeless Youth Program.* Washington, DC: U.S. Government Printing Office.

U.S. Department of Health and Human Services. (1999b). *Runaway and homeless youth: FY 1998 annual report to Congress.* Washington, DC: Administration for Children Youth and Families, Family and Youth Services Bureau.

U.S. House of Representatives, Education and Labor Committee. (1992). Legislative history, juvenile justice and delinquency amendments. *U.S. Code of Law and Administrative News,* House Report No. 102–756.

Waldfogel, J. (2000). Reforming child protective services. *Child Welfare, 69,* 43–57.

Wallace, J. I., & Weiner, A. (1994). [Foundation for Research on Sexually Transmitted Diseases, Inc.]. Unpublished data.

Whitbeck, L. B., & Hoyt, D. R. (1999). *Nowhere to grow: Homeless and runaway adolescents and their families.* Hawthorne, NY: Aldine de Gruyter.

Whitbeck, L. B., Hoyt, D. R., & Ackley, K. A. (1997a). Abusive family backgrounds and later victimization among runaway and homeless adolescents. *Journal of Research on Adolescence, 7,* 375–392.

Whitbeck, L. B., Hoyt, D. R., & Ackley, K. A. (1997b). Families of homeless and runaway adolescents: A comparison of parent/caretaker and adolescent perspectives on parenting, family violence, and adolescent conduct. *Child Abuse and Neglect, 21,* 517–528.

Whitbeck, L. B., & Simons, R. L. (1990). Life on the streets: The victimization of runaway and homeless adolescents. *Youth and Society, 22,* 108–125.

Williams, R. J., & Chang, S. Y. (2000). A comprehensive and comparative review of adolescent substance abuse treatment outcome. *Clinical Psychology: Science and Practice, 7* (2), 138–166.

Wright, J. D. (1989). *Poverty, homelessness, health, nutrition, and children.* Paper delivered at the Conference on Homeless Children and Youth: Coping with a National Tragedy, Washington, DC.

Wright, J. D. (1991). Children in and of the streets. Health, social policy and the homeless young. *American Journal of Diseases of Children, 145,* 516–519.

Yates, G. L., MacKenzie, R., Pennbridge, J., & Cohen, E. (1988). A risk profile comparison of runaway and non-runaway youth. *American Journal of Public Health, 78,* 820–821.

Yoder, K. A. (1999). Comparing suicide attempters, suicide ideators, and non-suicidal homeless and runaway adolescents. *Suicide and Life-Threatening Behaviors, 29,* 25–36.

Zlotnick, C., Robertson, M. J., & Wright, M. A. (1999). The impact of childhood foster care and other out-of-home placement on homeless women and their children. *Child Abuse and Neglect, 23,* 1057–1068.

INDEX

About the Author

NATASHA SLESNICK is Director of the Runaway and Homeless Youth Program at the University of New Mexico. She is the principal investigator on five federally funded projects to evaluate and develop treatments for the youths and their families. Slesnick is also a Research Associate Professor of Psychology at the University of New Mexico and Associate Director of the Clinical Research Branch at the UNM Center on Alcoholism, Substance Abuse, and Addictions.

DATE			